THE COMPLETE GUIDE TO TURKEY TAXIDERMY

THE COMPLETE GUIDE TO TURKEY TAXIDERMY

How to Prepare Fans, Beards, and Body Mounts

Todd Triplett

The Lyons Press
Guilford, Connecticut
An imprint of The Globe Pequot Press

Dedication

This book is dedicated to my best friend Sherry. Without her encouragement my dream of becoming an outdoor writer may not have been achieved.

The Lyons Press is an imprint of The Globe Pequot Press.

Printed in the United States of America

Designed by Compset, Inc.

10 9 8 7 6 5 4 3 2 1

Library of Congress Cataloging-in-Publication Data is available on file.

ISBN 1-58574-853-6

Contents

Acknowledgments

Thanks go out to the many influences that I have had throughout my life.

My grandfather, Jesse Triplett, who initialized my love for the great outdoors. My father, Larry Triplett, who influenced my desire to become a taxidermist. And my friend, Junior Bryant, who helped to guide and refine my taxidermy experience.

Also, thanks go out to my many friends within the writing industry, who were there to offer assistance and support.

Introduction

I became hooked on turkey hunting many years ago. It didn't take long from that first successful hunt for an eastern turkey to acquire the desire to obtain and mount each of the four major subspecies that live throughout the country: Eastern, Florida (Osceola), Merriam's, and Rio Grande. A few years passed before I had the means to complete a long-distance hunt for the other subspecies.

After a 30-hour drive my desires were about to become reality. My best friend, Sherry, and I were on the Pine Ridge Indian Reservation in southwestern South Dakota. The reason for our visit was simple. We hoped to harvest one of the many Merriam's turkeys that inhabited the area.

We quickly located several birds that first evening. After hearing numerous gobbles it was evident we would be in for a treat come sunrise. We returned to camp with high expectations for a productive morning hunt.

The smell of cooking steak soon filled the air as we prepared our evening meal. We deliberated about who would shoot first and what we would do with our birds. To say the least, we were confident. The cool, early-spring air mixed well with the yips and howls of the occasional coyote. It was a beautiful evening. The one-inch-thick rib eyes and potatoes were charcoaled to perfection, and we had good company, good weather, no cares or worries, just birds and lots of 'em. We drifted off that night talking about—what else—longbeards. A perfect ending to a perfect day.

In just six hours we were awakened by the annoying sound of a travel alarm clock. Sitting up in my sleeping bag, I scratched my head and thought, "Who in their right mind would do this for a bird?" That thought soon diminished as we began to move around, preparing for our hunt. We sucked down breakfast, then pulled on our camo gear.

Grabbing scatterguns and vests we wasted no time getting underway. We hurried along the dirt road as the sky in the east began to lighten. Getting closer to our destination, we slowed the pace, trying to listen for any activity. Only seconds after leaving the road's dusty surface a group of birds sounded off, then another, and another.

With as much stealth as possible, we located perfect places to sit where we could watch a small meadow along the creek bottom. While listening to the anxious birds, some up the creek and some down, we whispered our plans. Because we had never doubled on birds, we decided that if the opportunity presented itself to take legal gobblers we would take it, no matter the size. Further plans determined shooting sequence; I would yelp, then one, two, three, shoot.

With a few final squirms we found comfortable positions to wait, then stayed still. Several minutes passed before I began my plea for some company. *Yelp, yelp*—that's all it took. *Gobble!* As the eager toms voiced their desire to find a willing hen, I shifted my blackpowder shotgun, a new Knight TK-2000, in their direction. When I called again, the overzealous birds cut me off. Things were fixing to get interesting.

Several minutes passed while the birds gobbled and made their way up the narrow creek bottom. Knowing what I did about birds, I remained silent—playing hard to get. Soon, we heard footsteps in the leaves, which only added to our excitement.

All of our attention was directed toward the crunching leaves. Then, ever so cautiously, like burglars entering a home, one, then two, then two more redheads crested a small knoll within shooting distance. The four jakes had traveled a small gully to within 25 yards of us. Once the arrogant juveniles could see the length of the small meadow, they again called for their lady. But the only response they received was an inquisitive yelp, then three seconds of silence before our shotguns bellowed.

At the sound of the blast the would-be suitors made a hasty getaway, leaving two of their siblings flapping on the ground. Running to grab our prizes, we high-fived, hugged, and back-slapped. We had just created a memory neither of us would ever forget.

We took our time field dressing our trophies, simply enjoying God's creation and each other's company. When our chore was complete, we hiked back to camp with the birds draped across our shoulders.

We spoke of the morning's events as we walked, and our thoughts turned to what we wanted to do with this portion of our

Turkeys taken together on Pine Ridge Indian Reservation.

turkey grand slam. Because we already had several birds mounted life-size, we opted to take a quality photo and then mount the fans together, as that was how they were harvested. Preserving those fans and taking a picture helped us remember that day. Although the memories would always be with us, without those records they would someday fade.

While I had always held the wild turkey to be a beautiful creature rivaled by no other, this admiration greatly increased as hunts like the one above began to accumulate. And once the hunts were over, they were all worthy of preservation to some degree.

As my experience as a taxidermist grew, I noticed that no book completely covered all aspects of turkey taxidermy. Sure, there were plenty of books on the market with generalized instructions for mounting birds, fish, or big game, but none centered on this majestic bird. So I decided to pass along some of the techniques I have been fortunate enough to learn in my years as a turkey hunter and taxidermist. Most of the techniques in this book are ones that

Closeups can later yield good reference.

experience has shown me to be the simplest. You will quickly find there are many different viable techniques within taxidermy. In no way is this book intended to be the know-all, be-all, but the procedures presented here are time-tested and produce quality results.

Whether you are setting out to become a world-class taxidermist or simply to learn more about properly mounting a fan, there is something here for you. Having more knowledge about what it takes to achieve the greatest possible results is what it is all about. Within these pages, you will find information on everything from proper field care to how to make a quality fan of your own to how to become a competitive, professional taxidermist.

This book is for hunters whose hearts quicken at the sound of a gobble or those who walk mile after mile in search of a chess match with a spring monarch or those who marvel at the sight of a strutting bird laden with bronze and iridescent greens, golds, and blues. It is for those who yearn for the satisfying weight of a bird over the shoulder as they tramp from the field and those who simply love this beautiful bird and want to become more involved with preserving its beauty.

Almost Lost

Had it not been for individual state agencies, devoted hunters, and the National Wild Turkey Federation (NWTF), we might not even have the opportunity to harvest this bird—which I consider the greatest gamebird. The NWTF was founded in 1973. At that time there were an estimated 1.3 million wild turkeys and 1.5 million turkey hunters. NWTF volunteers and partners worked diligently with wildlife agencies to help reestablish flocks that had long been depleted. Today, there are 5.6 million wild turkeys and approximately 2.6 million turkey hunters. Since 1985, the NWTF and cooperating agencies have spent more than $150 million on over 20,000 projects benefiting wild turkeys throughout North America. The only state that currently doesn't have a huntable population of turkeys is Alaska, primarily due to its harsh climate. To join the National Wild Turkey Federation, call 1-800-THE-NWTF or visit their website at www.nwtf.org.

1

Field Care

I have taken in some horribly cared for turkeys that were to be mounted over the years. The hunters just didn't understand the need for proper field care. In some cases, the lucky hunter thought the best thing to do was to give the bird a good stomp on the head as it made those last death-throe flops. Worse yet, some have felt the need for a "finishing shot." These can do considerable damage, as most are at point-blank range. But it doesn't stop there. I have taken in birds that were shoved into the freezer any way possible, leaving tails shaped like question marks, right angles, or even S-curves. Many were just shot and shot hard. When these harsh actions are taken, it obviously creates a tougher job for the person chosen to re-create this beautiful bird. Often, the average hunter doesn't even give a second thought to the bird's condition.

The goal of any turkey hunter looking to preserve a trophy should be to achieve the most impressive mount possible. This begins with proper care in the field and should continue throughout the mounting process. Proper field care actually begins with proper preparation and planning before the harvest takes place. Even the most skilled taxidermist will be frustrated while dealing with a bird that is poorly cared for. And trying to learn taxidermy on a less-than-perfect specimen will be nothing short of a disaster.

Most hunters know whether they hope to preserve their prize before ever venturing afield. In addition to determining the desire for a mount, it is best to have at least a general idea of the likely pose as well as the location chosen for placing this work of art. This allows the hunter to be extra cautious when dealing with certain areas of the turkey. If a flying pose is chosen, the back, tail, and wing feathers should be closely cared for. If a fan is chosen, obviously the tail is your only major concern. Hunters may go several

1

seasons between harvests, so it is particularly important to take the extra steps in obtaining a trophy in top shape for the desired mount.

Accidents may occur even with proper knowledge and preparation. A couple of years back, a fellow hunter who had never taken a wild turkey filled his first tag. Immediately following the shot the hunter and a buddy ran to the bird. In all of the excitement, one of them stepped on the bird's tail. The bird gave one last flop and all the tail feathers were jerked free. This was a freak occurrence, but the hunter should be aware of his surroundings at all times. As far as I know, the lucky—then unlucky—hunter who hoped to mount his first bird was able to do nothing with his damaged prize, and to this day he hasn't been fortunate enough to harvest another.

Simple rules for bringing home a prime candidate for a taxidermy project include limiting feather loss, keeping the plumage free of any fluids (including water or body fluids), and cooling the bird as soon as possible.

Avoiding feather loss can sometimes be tricky due to the two ounces of lead most often used to harvest a gobbler. A poorly placed shot can wreak havoc on an otherwise perfect bird, but the hunter can take precautions that will help considerably. Although it is sometimes tough to keep your wits when a gobbler comes strutting in, gobbling the entire distance, maintaining a rational strategy often results in a cleaner kill with less damage.

To prevent major feather loss from the shot, don't let the bird get too close. This isn't usually a problem with these wary creatures, but occasionally we hunters get carried away with the beauty of such a sight and before we even realize it our prey is within spitting distance. It is best to snuff a gobbler at around the 30-yard mark. The shotgun's pattern is usually wide enough to avoid a direct hit to only one area of feathers at this medium distance. I have taken in many gobblers that looked as if they had been hit by a truck—a big truck. This is usually due to a very close shot or multiple shots. These birds can be repaired, but it is time-consuming and the results are usually less than perfect.

Almost any repair can be made using healthy feather tracts from other skins, but it makes for a tougher job, especially for a novice. While all feathers are important, the tail and wing primaries are probably the most noticeable. These feathers are particularly vulnerable while a turkey is in full strut, as all are extended. If possible, avoid shooting a gobbler while he is in full strut. If a bird seems re-luctant to break strut, give a sharp cluck; even the most excited bird will usually "periscope up" to find what he believes to be a new girlfriend. A well-placed shot in the head area of a standing gobbler at a moderate distance will most often result in a clean kill with few lost or damaged feathers.

While the bird will be washed at a later time, it is best to main-tain a completely dry trophy in the field. Blood, as well as most body fluids, contain proteins that are difficult to completely remove without chemicals or harsh washing. Wetness also comprises half the ingredients for unwanted bacteria growth. To avoid getting blood on the feathers, take along cotton swabs and plug every ori-fice. These include the mouth, anal opening, and any major shot holes. If the bird is bleeding excessively from the head, it is wise to wrap the skin area with tissue. This will help prevent blood from getting onto the smaller neck feathers, which are more vulnerable to damage. Certain circumstances are unavoidable. If you happen to get caught in a downpour or your bird flops into a creek, the best thing to do is either skin, flesh, wash, degrease, and dry the feathers right away or get the bird into the freezer immediately. I don't like to freeze a wet bird, though. This is because the feathers have a shape memory. If the bird is frozen wet the feathers never seem to regain their natural shape and fullness.

Another key area that has long been neglected by otherwise knowledgeable sportsmen is getting a properly dried bird to the freezer as quickly as possible. Birds have higher body temperatures than other game, and because of the good insulating qualities of their feathers they hold this heat much longer. Unfortunately, heat and moisture are prime breeding grounds for bacteria, which is enemy number one to the taxidermist. Even an otherwise properly cared for turkey with very few damaged feathers can be lost due to slippage from bacteria build-up. It is completely understandable that a successful hunter wants to show a trophy to hunting buddies or co-workers, but this can be detrimental to any game that is to be mounted. To avoid this problem and still be able to boast, take sev-eral quality pictures, go to a one-hour photo center, and then visit everyone.

One more rule to follow is to skip the field dressing. I am usu-ally a fanatic for field dressing any game, but field dressing a bird destined for taxidermy usually creates more problems than it solves.

By opening up the bird in the field, more blood and fluids will be released to contaminate the feathers. The small feathers around the vent area are more susceptible to collecting debris, and they are also some of the toughest to clean properly.

Once a bird is harvested and proper field-care guidelines have been followed, you are almost finished. If you have time to start work immediately on the mount, do so. If not, proper storage should be a priority at this point. Upon getting to a freezer, arrange an unobstructed area in which to lay the turkey. Avoid bending the feathers, and don't place anything on top of the bird, which may break feathers. Do not put the bird into a plastic bag right away, as this will help retain heat and may create moisture problems if the bird is still warm. Place the bird in the freezer without a bag for at least an hour, then remove and double bag it to keep other freezer contaminants from getting on the bird. If freezer space is an issue, skin the bird then place it in the freezer.

If proper care is administered during the entire process prior to mounting, you should be rewarded with a mount of higher quality that is a pleasure to work with.

Tools

The outcome is better and the work more enjoyable during any job when the right tools are available throughout the process. Some tools of the taxidermy trade can be pricey, but in the long run they are worth their weight in gold. In the initial learning stages, all the tools may not be absolutely necessary, but having them will make certain tasks much simpler. What follows is a description of each tool, what its duties are, and, in my opinion, whether it is optional or not.

Latex Surgical Gloves. I have seen numerous taxidermists who neglected to use gloves of any kind while handling birds and mammals that were to be mounted. Their reason for being so careless was usually, "I can't feel my work as well." In my opinion, an opinion shared by others in the field who have seen firsthand the devastating effect of not wearing protective gear, this is without doubt a health bomb waiting to go off. When it comes to the issue of gloves, the only question should be, "What size do I need?" This item is definitely not optional.

While most diseases prevalent in the animal kingdom can't be passed to humans, some can. Rabies is probably at the top of the list. I know many taxidermists who will not even accept raccoons or foxes. Though the chances of ever coming in contact with a bird or animal that has a transmittable disease is probably somewhere between slim and none, once it occurs it's too late to consider the options.

Scalpel. This may be the most-used tool of the taxidermy trade. The scalpel's duties should be obvious; it is used to skin all birds and mammals. And while many hunters insist on a knife for skinning, buying scalpels negates the need for regular sharpening. Scalpels are also much sharper than a knife sharpened by hand.

Scalpels can be used alone, but they are best suited for attachment to a scalpel handle. Although small plastic scalpel handles are available, I would advise investing the extra couple dollars for a weighted, stainless steel handle. The weight helps the scalpel to sit nicely in one hand while work is performed.

Be extra cautious when using scalpels. Even the poorest grades are razor-sharp, and if a careless slip is made you may end up with stitches to remind you of this fact. Scalpels are optional but much more effective than a knife.

Scissors. Small curved scissors can be used to help with the de-fatting process. When fat or muscle tissue is very thin, holding a pair of these small inexpensive scissors tight against the skin will seem invaluable. Scissors are optional.

Bird Flesher. As you will quickly find out, the turkey is a fatty bird, second only to ducks and geese. To complete a quality mount, virtually all of this fat must be removed. Some taxidermists take great pains with scissors, scalpels, and knives, but the skin is usually not as clean as it would be when de-fatted in conjunction with a wire-wheeled bird flesher. These machines usually start at about $150 and up, but a quality flesher will soon pay for itself with the reduction of time it takes to de-fat a bird. This would be a worthy investment for almost anyone who intends to take up taxidermy as a hobby or occupation. While the wheel was designed for birds, it also lends itself well to small mammals. Some may consider the wire flesher optional, but I consider it a must-have.

Bondo. It may seem strange to include what is considered an automotive adhesive on the list, but the fact is that without bondo the taxidermy world would be scrambling for an exact substitute. Bondo has many uses in the taxidermy shop, including manikin repair, securing the base of a spread turkey tail, attaching artificial fish heads, attaching antlers to big game, and so on. When purchasing bondo, no special formula is needed; any kind you can pick up at a convenience store or automotive store will do.

Wire. Wire is used to position an otherwise limp bird. Turkeys require many different sizes, with most ranging from 8 to 12 or 14 gauge, depending on preference. Once you mount a couple of birds, you may prefer a certain gauge wire. There is no set standard, only good starting points. Wire is not optional.

Thread and Needles. Thread will be used to sew up any incisions made in the turkey. No special thread is needed, although I prefer to use a dark colored thread that will easily hide in the dark feathers. Taxidermy suppliers sell a black, fine, unwaxed, thread that is great for any sewing. Upholstery thread sold at most convenience stores will also work.

Needles best suited for turkey sewing are long (usually two to four inches) and small in diameter. The goal here is not a sturdy needle, but one that is easy to locate. A small needle will tend to be lost among the thick feathers of a turkey. A round needle, rather than the tri-cut versions, is best suited for the tender skin of the turkey. The tri-cut needles are excellent for thicker skinned game, but can cause bird skin to rip easily.

Turkey Manikins. Many years ago, everyone who performed taxidermy would wrap their own bodies. This meant mashing and twisting excelsior into a shape resembling the bird body. Once a generic shape was achieved, they would wrap twine around the mass to help hold it.

As everything does, taxidermy evolved, and top taxidermists around the country began studying birds very closely and taking very accurate measurements. After casting, measuring, and studying thousands of specimens they began producing bird manikins. Bird manikins consist of the same hard foam that is found in all mammal manikins, but they resemble a bird carcass almost exactly. These are highly recommended, especially for learning or commercial purposes. Their top qualities include anatomical accuracy and holding wire well, and most have the position for the wing and leg wire pre-marked. This is critical, because a discrepancy of only half an inch from where a wire belongs could be devastating to the final product.

The art of wrapping and carving bodies is alive and well, and if a person plans to practice bird taxidermy to any extent they should learn this important procedure. It is the only alternative when the taxidermist encounters a unique or oddly-shaped bird. These techniques are also the choice of many world champions, as they will be more accurate from a competitive standpoint.

Although manikins are optional, they are tremendous time-savers.

Degreaser. Proper degreasing is very important when dealing with any fatty bird or animal. To assure a quality, long-lasting mount, it is very important that you degrease the skin properly. This can mean the difference between a good-looking mount that will be with you for many years and one that starts off poorly and deteriorates quickly. A good example of poor fleshing and degreasing is an older duck mount that has started to yellow. (I use a duck mount in this example because they are probably the toughest to flesh properly, and due to their colors the grease bleed will be more noticeable.)

Several methods exist for proper degreasing. Many top taxidermists swear by Dawn dishwashing liquid, claiming it is their only degreaser. I have used Dawn alone in the past, but now I prefer to use it in conjunction with a commercial degreaser. I find that when using a commercial degreaser my birds feel much cleaner, dry more quickly, and are shinier.

Dry Preservative or Bird Tan. A quality dry preservative or quality bird tan will help ensure that no bugs eat away at your creation. Most world-class bird taxidermists use dry preservative. It is quick and easy, but newer bird tans can be just as quick. For the beginner, dry preservative is probably the way to go. It is easy to apply with no special mixes. It is also easy to find; you can get borax at most grocery stores. If you are the experimental type, try different forms of preservative as your experience grows.

Tumbler. This is definitely the biggest ticket item on the supply list and, thankfully, probably the only truly optional one. Don't misunderstand optional as meaning not needed. A tumbler is a definite asset. The art of taxidermy can be performed without one, but it is a very helpful tool. The tumbler is a time-saver. Some wet birds can be deposited in the tumbler and after a short cycle come out virtually dry with only a slight touch-up needed before continuing the mounting procedure. The action of the tumbler also polishes the feathers, helping to enhance their luster.

Tumblers can be used in conjunction with various additives, with corncob grit and hardwood sawdust probably the most popular. For birds, only corncob grit should be used. Corncob grit comes in two sizes, coarse and fine. The fine grit is usually the only one used during bird taxidermy. The tumbler will be filled from a third to almost half full with this tumbling mix. Many taxidermists like to add other ingredients to their corncob grit. Some of the most popular are odorless mineral spirits, dry preservative, or both. Tumblers work well for cleaning and drying birds, and they work equally as well for mammal skins. So if you plan to make a hobby of taxidermy, learning to mount mammals as well as birds, the tumbler will be a good investment. The tumbler is optional, but the alternative is lengthy periods wielding a hair dryer.

Hair Dryer. The hair dryer is listed because you might want to get one to use exclusively for your new hobby. Although nothing is wrong with using the house hair dryer on birds, the lady of the house may have some preconceived notion that once it is used to dry turkey feathers it no longer will be suitable for her head. You can also score points here. Buy a new hair dryer and give it to your significant other as a gift. Then confiscate the old hair dryer.

I would recommend getting one that has an optional heat switch. You don't want to get a bird too hot, and having the ability to switch the heat off at any time is a plus. A hair dryer is not optional.

Regulator Needle. Regulator needles come in various lengths, and longer needles are best for bird taxidermy. Regulators are inexpensive, so you may want to buy several. From positioning feather tracts for pinning to layering individual feather rows and raising the back feathers on a strutting bird, the regulator needle has many uses. It is optional but very beneficial.

Neck Material. Initially, the novice taxidermist may choose to purchase pre-manufactured necks that attach nicely to the sculptor's own bodies. These pre-shaped necks take all the guesswork out of anatomy. This allows you to concentrate on the basics. If you choose to try it on your own, purchase neck material that is 1- to 1¼-inch in diameter. Neck material is cheap, so get 5 to 10 feet. This will allow you to experiment, and if you make a mistake you will have the appropriate materials with which to continue. Neck material isn't optional.

Polyfil or Cotton. Polyfil or cotton has several uses in bird taxidermy, and either works well. It can be used to wrap legs or wings, replacing the muscle tissue that was once there. It can also be used to help lock in the feathers along the back for birds in the strutting position. With any type of filler, a good rule of thumb to follow is not to use too much; you don't want the bird to look like it is on steroids. This is optional depending on personal techniques.

Liquid Preservative. While dry preservative or bird tan is effective on the skin, you will need a liquid preservative and a syringe for injecting portions of the wing and feet. These are usually unskinned areas that have little or no muscle tissue. Several types are available, and I have no constant favorites. A generic preservative preferred by many taxidermists is denatured alcohol, which is available at hardware stores. Mix the denatured alcohol equally with water and you have a capable liquid preservative. Liquid preservative is not an option.

Airbrush. Preservation methods in the taxidermy industry have made tremendous advances. So have the techniques used to add the natural colors that bring the finished product to life. Not so long ago, painting techniques involved paint brushes and automotive lacquers. The end result was usually suitable for the highly skilled, but often it was less than satisfactory for the beginner. In many cases, those first attempts were downright horrendous, causing a great deal of frustration during the learning process.

When taxidermists first attempted to work with airbrushes, probably sometime in the 1980s, they were able to perform fantastic work. About the time the airbrush was introduced, we also refined the paints that were used. Instead of borrowing paints from other trades, someone began specially formulating paints just for wildlife artistry. For the experienced taxidermist, these modern-day products can produce an incredible finished product. And for those just learning, it might shave months, if not years, from the time needed to create the same great results.

The airbrush is optional, but worth the minimal investment.

Air compressor. An air compressor is a great asset to the taxidermist. An air compressor isn't mandatory in bird taxidermy unless the beginner chooses to paint his own head.

A small version will work great for most purposes. Although a small one-horsepower with a two-gallon tank will suffice for painting, I would recommend at least a five-horsepower with a twenty-gallon tank. It is amazing how the workload will increase to include other heavier chores, either in the shop or for the home.

PUTTING IT ALL TOGETHER

Many supplies can be purchased through local retailers, but at some point you will have to contact a taxidermy supplier. It is the only way to purchase specialty equipment. One of the oldest taxidermy suppliers in the country is Van Dykes. They have helped taxidermists worldwide begin their hobbies and, for some, their careers. They have a vast assortment of nearly every type of taxidermy-related item available. Another benefit Van Dykes offers to its customers is technical advice from an on-staff taxidermist. Such advice can be priceless. Call 1-800-843-3320 or visit their website at www. vandykestaxidermy.com.

3

Reference and Anatomy

REFERENCE

All my life I have been amazed with the beauty of wildlife. I found the art derived from such wildlife just as amazing—whether it was photography, paintings, drawings, or taxidermy. But I was partial to artwork that involved actually re-creating the creature by hand. I thought there was some kind of secret or magic to drawing and taxidermy. How could someone know a turkey, deer, or bear so intimately and re-create it? Then, during my first trip to Yellowstone National Park, I found a major part of my answer.

I had always wanted to visit this extraordinary place, so full of wildlife and majestic scenery. Studying, photographing, and simply enjoying the abundant wildlife made up the bulk of my forays. At midday, as wildlife retreated to shade and privacy, I visited some of the natural wonders. Inside one of the information centers I found an artist painting an exceptional portrait of a buffalo. I eagerly watched, trying to learn something. Paying close attention, I began to notice that the artist would peer regularly through a small eyepiece on his workbench. After he did this several times, I asked him what he was looking at. He graciously offered me a look. I could see a photograph of a life-sized buffalo identical to the one being painted. Somewhat confused, I asked why he was constantly checking the photo. That's when he explained that all artists use reference material to duplicate anatomy, size, and other important features of their work. Understanding that fact cleared up a lot of unanswered questions for me. This same rule of reference applies to taxidermy.

When I began learning the art of taxidermy I again was taught the importance of reference, but had it not been for that experience in Yellowstone I might not have taken it as seriously. Without reference material our wildlife reproductions might more closely resemble a cartoon character rather than a living creature. The best taxidermists in the world constantly study and observe the species they intend to re-create. This speaks volumes. Although a taxidermist has competed in world taxidermy championships and probably has mounted hundreds, if not thousands, of turkeys, he will still constantly study and rely on his reference material for accurate re-creations.

Within the realm of reference material we have 2-D references, which include photographs and videos, and 3-D references, which include death masks and live specimens. All reference is valuable when preparing to mount, and it is not a good idea to rely on just one form of reference.

A word of caution here: Don't use others' mounted birds as reference. It is fine to study another's work. It is even recommended. Studying the work of others may help with technique improvement, but a mount is the taxidermist's own idea of what a creature should look like. It isn't necessarily 100 percent accurate for a live animal. It is an individual's perception of that creature. Nothing will replace a live specimen.

To study properly you must first obtain proper reference materials. These materials are among the cheapest tools we can acquire. If you think a reference source isn't readily available, just look under your nose. For instance, if you want to mount your own turkey, you are probably a hunter. Every turkey hunter I know has a number of hunting videos lying around. Also, unless I am the only one, most hunters have accumulated stacks of hunting magazines through the years.

Magazines such as the NWTF's *Turkey Call* or *Turkey* and *Turkey Hunting* are packed full of great color photos each month. Other magazines occasionally will have turkey photos, but the two just mentioned are devoted solely to the wild turkey.

If you desire closer shots or more precise pictures, a full selection is available at most taxidermy suppliers. These photos will have high quality close-ups of individual areas. I highly recommend getting at least one booklet from a qualified reference photographer, as well as all the other free photos you can acquire.

An ideal way to begin a reference library is to get several folders and label the contents. A good example might be a folder full of strutting photos, or another full of gobbling birds, or another full of turkey heads—the list goes on and on. Once a magazine is retired, sift through it and cut out the photos you need and then toss the remains. This will serve two purposes. It will offer you lifelong reference material and it will appease a less-than-understanding spouse who doesn't like piles of old magazines lying around.

The ultimate reference is a live bird. Ideally, the taxidermist would have ready access to an aviary for reference study. If we were talking about smaller upland birds or even waterfowl this feat might be more easily accomplished, but turkeys are large birds and require large living areas. All is not lost, though. If you live in a rural area there might be the possibility of constructing a small pen for a gobbler and a hen. Turkeys are available through farmers and many will have traditional colored feathers that duplicate those of a wild bird. And what turkey hunter doesn't thrill to the sound of a gobble at first light?

If a personal aviary is out of the question, other options remain. A library of videos is great. Most hunting videos show turkeys as they cautiously make their way to the hunter. Great footage of strutting, gobbling, and walking turkeys abound in these hunting videos, and if the hunter misses you may even see one flying.

Additional reference can be gained from your own hunting experiences. Once you familiarize yourself with what to look for, it is amazing what you will notice when watching wildlife. Something as simple as a slight color change in the head as the turkey's moods change or the position of the head as the bird struts; such previously unnoticed details become more apparent.

Earlier, I noted that a good 3-D reference is the death mask. Although a turkey taxidermist doesn't necessarily need a death mask, it is important to know what it is. A death mask is a reproduction of a particular part of anatomy. For example, death masks are often made of waterfowl skulls, big game noses, and big game eyes (the entire area around the eye). The death mask is seldom used in turkey taxidermy because there are few taxidermists who mount their own turkey heads. Most use a reproduction or freeze-dried version. I consider these to be the best methods, as well. I wouldn't recommend conventionally mounting a turkey head, but if you want to try mounting the turkey head naturally a quality cast or reproduction can be a tremendous asset for determining angles of the neck and head, along with the fullness of the fleshy skin. After compiling some material, you will be ready to start learning how to read and better understand this road map to a lifelike mount.

To better understand the importance of reference you must first understand a person's inclinations in how he or she views a picture. If you show a picture of a strutting turkey to an individual untrained in reading reference and ask them what they see, they will likely respond that they see a turkey. Although this statement isn't wrong, it isn't the answer we are looking for. Ask the same question of one trained to view and understand reference, and they will likely respond with comments about the location of each individual feather tract. They also may make reference to the angle of the legs or the head. Many of these individual details may be rattled off before they are finished.

To do a competent job as a taxidermist you must break down a picture while studying it. Instead of looking at a picture as a whole, you must learn to notice each detail of your study piece. An excellent way to learn this is to use straight lines within a box to better understand angles and shapes that are pertinent to the re-creation of a subject. I have found a good tool to be a piece of paper with a small rectangular hole cut in it. The size of the box will depend on the size of the photo you are working with; the smaller the photo the smaller the box. To use this tool, take a picture of a standing turkey and use the small box to separate an individual area that you would like to learn more about. Let's use the wings. As you box off the wings, lay a straightedge horizontally or vertically across the opening. You will quickly see angles and shapes that were previously unnoticed. This will help in the proper positioning of the final mount. Another example might be to box off the chest area of a strutting turkey. You should immediately notice the individual feather tracts as they come together in the front. By using the straightedge, you will get a better understanding of where the feather tracts should begin and end. You will also understand what angle the feather tracts take along the body. The uses of this cut out are limitless and can be very helpful to anyone trying to learn minute details about their subject.

As a taxidermist, your goal should be to perfectly duplicate the specimen you are re-creating. This task is virtually impossible if you are not intimately familiar with the specimen you have chosen; in this case, the turkey. As your experience grows, your taxidermy skills will increase and so will your ability to understand and interpret reference. Skills learned here will lend themselves to other areas of taxidermy as well.

ANATOMY

For our purposes, anatomy is defined as the structure of a given animal. This includes both the muscle and skeletal structure of a turkey. Anatomical understanding is very important to the aspiring taxidermist. Some may think that this study is best left to sculptors who spend countless hours studying and reproducing anatomy. It is also true that most of the skeletal and muscular reproduction is handled for you by today's modern manikins. However, who is to say the sculptor didn't make a mistake. Besides, learning as much as possible about a subject will help us to re-create it more naturally.

How would it look if we mounted a turkey with a wing sticking from its back and a leg on its side? The thought alone is rather comical. Although you may not make this large a mistake while performing taxidermy, without a better understanding of anatomy, you may complete a project that looks unnatural. This is especially true if you neglect to learn as much as possible about the anatomy of your chosen species.

When doing big game taxidermy it is a bit easier to get away with a less than perfect understanding of anatomy. This is because the manikins produced for big game already include the body, neck, head, and legs (if doing a life-sized mount). Bird taxidermists don't have that advantage, though. Most often, the only part that is pre-sculpted is the body. We have to complete the project by attaching the legs and wings in the appropriate places. Also, the neck has to be made and attached. In recent years some pre-sculpted parts, including necks, drumsticks, and wings, have entered the market. You still shouldn't allow this to lessen your desire to learn about anatomy.

Anatomy isn't one of those subjects that you can fully understand in just a few paragraphs or a few hours, but if you understand the basics you will learn quickly as you do more research and tackle more projects. An excellent opportunity for learning more about anatomy is during the skinning process. By working with a specimen before skinning begins you can get a better understanding of that species. Before any skinning takes place it is easy to swivel and bend a turkey's wings or legs and assess other variables to get an idea about range of motion. A good example if the importance of this study is that before a turkey is skinned you will only be able to bend its wing so far in any direction before a ligament or muscle group stops the movement. Once the muscles are removed, you can flex the wing past this natural point, although it wouldn't be natural.

Notice how each bone is attached to the next while skinning the turkey. Also important is how the muscles attach and hold the bones. This is a never-ending learning process. Even today I will learn something new while skinning an animal or bird. By making mental notes of how all the parts go together you will quickly begin to understand what is natural and what isn't, and that is what taxidermy is all about—natural duplication.

CHAPTER 4

Skinning

Before you begin to skin a turkey for the mounting process it is important to know what pose will likely be used. Some methods of skinning are more conducive to particular mounts. Several incisions can be used, but the most popular are the breast incision and the leg-to-leg incision. Either will work, but as you learn more you will eventually prefer one method over the other. I prefer the leg-to-leg. This skinning method reduces the exposure of the feathers to the fatty area of the breast. But the breast incision is great because it offers much more room to work. Other methods include a side incision and a back, or dorsal, incision. These are used infrequently, but it is good to know that they exist should the need arise.

If you have placed your trophy in the freezer for storage it is best to let it begin to thaw. This helps to alleviate the problem of tearing skin. Proper thawing also makes the work much easier. You will quickly find out that birds of any species are well insulated. I have removed turkeys from the freezer to mount in the warmer months of June and July, and they were still too frozen to efficiently work with 24 hours later. So it is very important to make the proper arrangements if your plan is to work on a frozen bird. Even unfleshed, unpreserved skins pulled from the freezer will take a bit longer to thaw than you realize.

Although skinning can be messy, as with all other processes, it is best to maintain a clean, dry bird. The first thing to do is prepare the work area. You should start with a clean, dry surface. I have found that freezer paper works great for this. Pull off a couple lengths and tack them into place and your workbench is ready. And as an added bonus it will be a simple chore to clean up once the skinning job is complete. Freezer paper isn't a must, but it is inexpensive and readily available. In addition to the freezer paper, I like to generously sprinkle a bed of dry preservative (borax will work) on which to lay the bird. This is to soak up any lost fluids. Otherwise, you might be rolling the bird around in a terrible mess that will hinder the final product.

After the skinning table is ready it is usually best to have all the necessary tools laid out within easy reach. This is primarily for time management, as you will find things go much faster when the required tools are handy. I also keep a supply of dry preservative nearby to soak up any body fluids that seep onto dry feathers during the skinning process. Keeping a bird as clean and dry as possible before the washing process will pay huge dividends in the end result.

Another decision that needs to be made now is whether to remove the head prior to or after the skinning process. Those who advocate removing the head prior to skinning say that the head is usually the first area to thaw. Therefore, they recommend going ahead with removal and preparation for the freeze drier. This will guarantee the freshest head possible, lessening any deterioration that may take place.

I feel removing the head prior to skinning does more harm than good. The feathers along the neck area next to the head are probably the most sensitive feathers on the bird. They are easily damaged and difficult to clean. For this reason, I avoid removing the head until after skinning so that I'm less likely to taint these sensitive feathers with blood and other fluids. Also, my experience has shown that removing the head and hanging the turkey upside down may just be asking for trouble. It is easy to understand that once the turkey is hanging, any fluids will drain. As they reach the neck area the small feathers act as a wick, absorbing the wetness.

As an extra precaution, I wrap the turkey head before beginning the skinning process. (A paper towel works great for this.) This helps prevent the tainting of feathers due to any fluids lost during the skinning process.

REMOVING THE TAIL SECTION PRIOR TO SKINNING

Some taxidermists consider it difficult to remove the tail prior to skinning, but I like to do it before making any incisions because it gets the fragile tail out of the way before possible damage can occur.

To start, raise the secondary feathers, the ones closest to the tail, which consist of the large primary feathers. Now take the scalpel and cut parallel with the tail section, raising the back skin as you make the cut. You should cut well into this tail section to assure that the ends of the quills are free. Now make a similar cut on the underside next to the primaries. After the cuts are complete, connect them on each end and gently begin freeing the tail from the carcass. Once free, set the tail aside and continue with the skinning process.

BREAST INCISION

Begin by laying the bird on its back. It may have a tendency to roll to one side or the other. You should easily be able to adapt to this situation, but if rolling is a problem you can build a small V-shaped structure that will hold the bird upright until the initial incisions are complete.

With the bird on its back, locate the point of the breastbone midway up the body. This should be easily found. The skin on the breast point is usually tough compared to the rest of the skin, so be sure not to cut past this area. If you do, it will make the skin more likely to tear. I like to cut an X on this breast point. This helps with realigning the skin during mounting should you tear it during the remainder of the skinning and fleshing procedures. Now locate the anal opening; it will be easily found near the base of the tail primaries.

Once both of these points are found, use a regulator or thin wire to separate the feathers along the breast. Between these feathers, in the very center of the breast, is an area that consists of only skin. The skin-only area will be approximately 1 inch wide. This area usually narrows as you reach the smaller feathers near the abdomen. After the skin area is found, use a scalpel to cut a line from the anal opening to the breast point and sprinkle the area with preservative. This will help soak up any fluids.

Next, start peeling back the skin. Remember, compared to other more fragile birds, turkey skin is not easily torn. But it is much easier to tear than most mammal skin. You can use the scalpel when trying to free the skin from the body at this beginning point. After

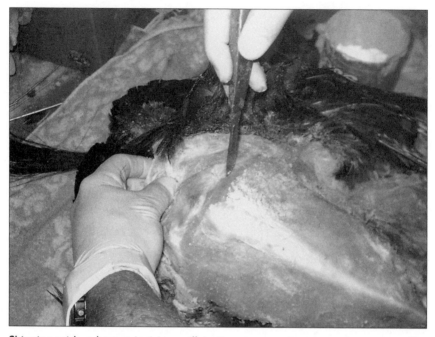

Skinning with a breast incision will invite more moisture to the surrounding feathers, but is a great way to learn.

getting started, you may find that it is much more effective to use only pressure from your hands to separate the skin from the body. This will help reduce the multiple holes caused by an overzealous scalpel blade.

After freeing the skin a couple of inches on either side of the incision area, begin working your hands between skin and carcass along either side of the body. You will ultimately want the skin to be loose from both sides. Generously apply dry preservative between the loose skin and muscle tissue underneath. Once the skin is loose on each side almost to the back area, start preparing the tail for separation from the body (if you didn't remove it before starting the skinning process).

Leg-to-Leg Incision

Beyond the initial cut, the leg-to-leg incision isn't very different from the breast incision. Just as the name implies, this incision is

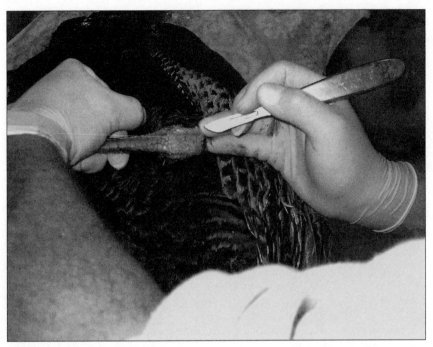

Before starting the leg-to-leg incision, cut cleanly around the joined area of the leg scales and feathers.

made from one leg to the other. There aren't any skin-only tracts as there were in the breast area, so you will just have to be very careful to avoid cutting any feathers.

Using the scalpel, cut from where the scales meet the feathers on one leg all the way across the abdomen to the same point on the opposite leg. I prefer this because the cut is in an area that has less fat than the breast, which helps reduce any tainting that may occur during skinning. Also, if these feathers are damaged by blood or oil they can be easily hidden.

After the cut is made, begin working the skin free towards the knee joint. Once the skin is loose, use the scalpel to cut through the femur-tibia joint. With each drumstick now free, begin freeing the skin along each thigh all the way to the back and to the base of the tail. If you haven't previously removed the tail, free the skin to just past the anal opening and on the back of the bird near the tail section. It may be easier to roll the bird onto its shoulders so the tail is pointing upwards. Bend the tail down towards the back and

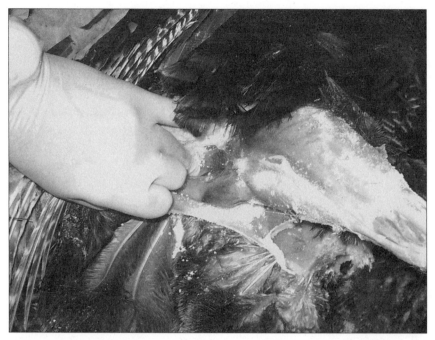

Using the leg-to-leg incision, peel the skin from the muscle tissue towards the outside of the thigh area.

begin cutting between the anal opening and the tail quills. As with the breast incision try to cut between two vertebrae to avoid dulling your scalpel or knife.

With the tail section free, work the skin along the back until it is loose well past the thigh area. You will also need to free the skin in the breast area to just past the breast point. Now you are ready to hang the bird and continue the skinning process.

REMOVING THE TAIL SECTION WITH THE SKIN, THEN SEPARATING

Some experienced taxidermists insist on leaving the tail attached to the body skin for the entire mounting process. I have found it much easier to separate the two. The skin isn't as awkward to handle, the tail section is less likely to be damaged during the skinning process, and the tail is easier to clean, spread, and position.

If you decided not to remove the tail before starting the skinning process, you can either remove it now or leave it attached and

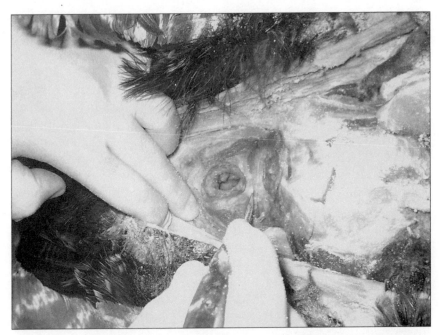

Initial cuts to remove the tail section will be very near the anal opening.

Cutting the tail section free should always be done very cautiously to avoid severing the back skin.

continue skinning. While it is not my preference, it initially may be easier to remove the skin with the tail attached. (If you would like to finish skinning with the tail attached to the body, skip ahead to the next step.)

To prepare the tail area for detachment now, continue loosening the skin rearward towards the base of the tail feathers. It is usually best to free the skin from the back area for at least an inch or more near the tail base. To do this, simply force your fingers around to the back. This will allow you to cut through the attached tail section without cutting holes in the cape. Try to avoid holes at all costs, but rest assured that most can be easily fixed, with very little visible evidence of the damaged area.

Continue freeing skin in the abdomen area until the skin is loose well past the anal opening. Once the skin between the tail section and anal opening is passed and the skin along the back free, begin cutting through the muscle tissue at the end of the spine. Again, try to cut between two vertebrae. This will make separation much easier. Once the tail section is cut free, you can continue with the skinning process.

THE REMAINDER OF THE SKINNING PROCESS

If you haven't already done so, continue loosening the skin on each side of the bird. When you reach the thigh area begin loosening the skin that is attached there, as well. Work your hands around to the back, freeing the skin to an area below the junction of the thigh and the drumstick (the thigh is properly called the femur and the drumstick the tibia). Now spread the legs so this area is more visible. You may have to exert a little pressure to do this, especially if the bird was previously frozen. Once this joint is visible, use the scalpel to cut the drumstick free from the thigh. This will take some getting used to. It is fine if you have to make several cuts, just be careful not to cut the skin.

When the joints on each leg are free, lay them beside your bird, out of the way. Continue working the skin free along the back, moving toward the front of the bird. After you have separated the skin far enough along the back, you will find skinning is much easier after hanging the carcass. To hang the bird, sharpen one end of a length of 8-gauge wire and then bend it into an S-shape. The wire

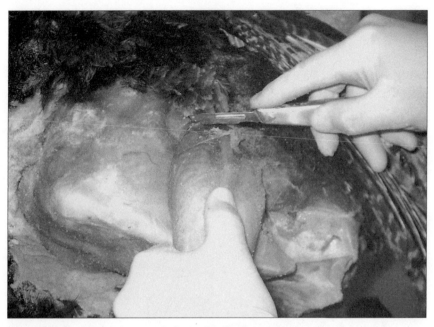

Beginning to cut the drumstick from the thigh.

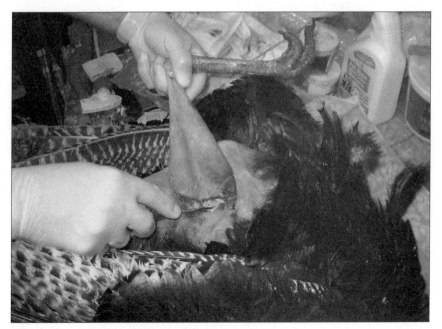

Side view of cutting the drumstick free.

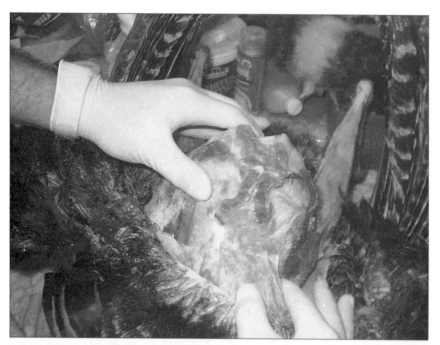

Start by working the skin loose along the back.

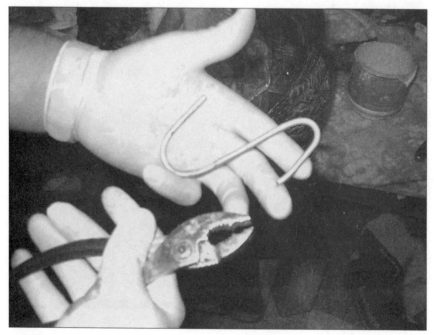

Shaping the hanging wire.

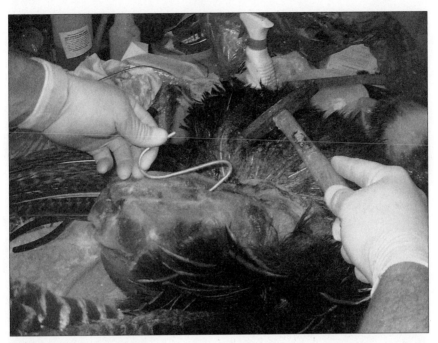

Inserting the hanging wire.

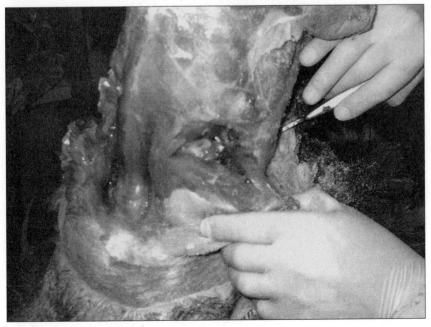

Cutting the wing free at the shoulder.

should resemble a hook on each end. With the wire in the desired shape, take the sharpened end and penetrate the carcass above the thigh area along the back. Then hang the bird about head high to continue the skinning process.

If the turkey is properly thawed the wings should gently droop toward the floor. If they don't, gently pull them down to allow easier access to the wing bone socket. Loosen the skin along the back toward the floor. Sometimes this skin is tough to separate with just your hands. If so, you may find it easier to use a scalpel.

Continue loosening the skin towards the neck area until the connection between the wing bone and the body is visible. Now, use a scalpel to cut the wing bone free from the body. After each wing bone is free it should fall easily out of the way. This will allow the skin to invert, which will make the final skinning much easier.

From this point, it is usually a simple matter of dusting the skin area with some preservative to ensure your grip and pulling the

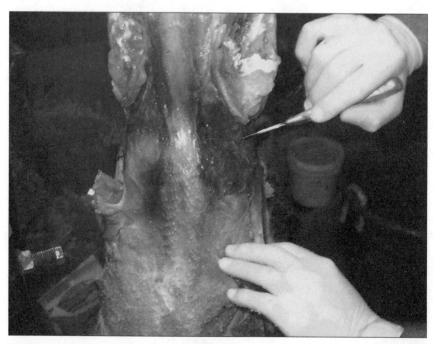

Continue skinning towards the head. Be very careful not to cut through the skin in this area.

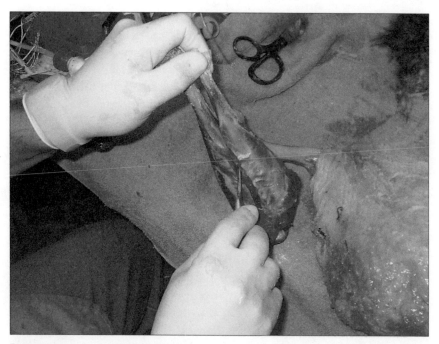

Removing tissue from the leg bone.

Do this only after tracing the actual size of the muscular tissue.

skin toward the head area. Gently work the skin free of the remaining carcass and continue along the neck. I try to free the skin almost all the way to the head. When you can't go any farther, sever the neck with a pair of snips.

Before inverting the skin to separate the head from the body, remove the muscle tissue that surrounds each drumstick and each wing bone.

To remove the drumstick muscle, make sure the skin is free almost the entire length of the tibia. Just above the joint where the feathers meet the skin you will find several tendons that attach the muscle to the tibia. Sever these, and use a knife to separate the leg muscle the entire length of the bone. Now you should have muscle tissue attached only to the ball. Using a pair of cutters, clip the bone adjacent to this ball. This will also sever any attached muscle tissue.

With the end cut free from the tibia, you should next clean the inside of the bone. To do this, insert a piece of large wire into the leg bone. This will force out any blood or fat.

The same goes for the wing bone. Cut the muscle tissue free from the elbow to the end of the wing bone. Using clippers or a

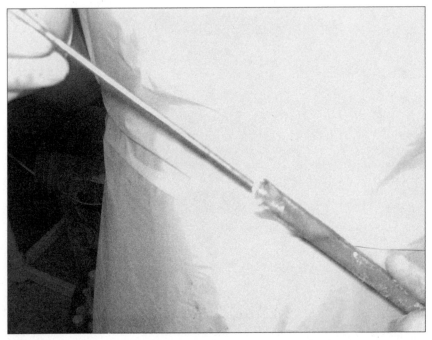

Using a large wire remove the marrow and fat within the leg bone.

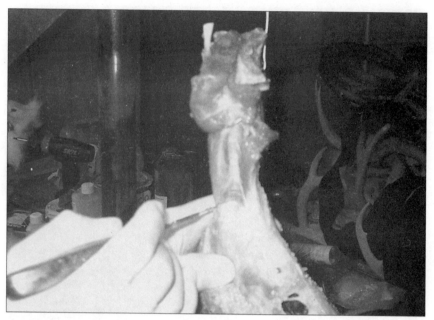

Skin the wing to the elbow, then remove the muscle.

knife, cut the muscle free from the wing bone. After each side is complete re-invert the skin.

If the tail hasn't already been removed, it should be done at this point. Remove the tail by looking at the inside of the skin to find

Cutting the tail free after the skin has been completely removed.

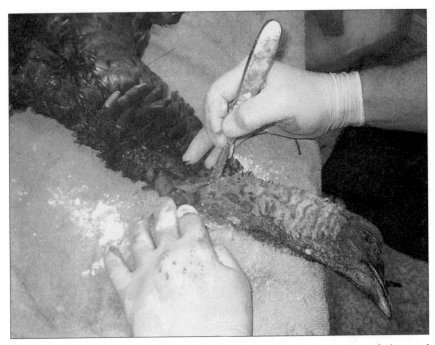

Carefully cut the head free along the line formed by the junction of skin and feathers.

the rows of feather quills. Cut between the feather rows about three rows from the tail. Make this cut all the way around, severing the tail from the skin. Once the tail is free, refer to chapter 7, Fan and Cape Preparation, for further instruction on how to properly flesh, clean, and position it for mounting.

With everything else complete, now is the ideal time to cut the head free from the skin. Lay the skin in a clean area, making sure that most feathers are in good shape and aren't being bent or broken. Hold the bird by the head and stretch it a bit. This should allow you to see the area where the skin meets feathers. If proper precautions have been taken the feathers along the neck should be virtually clean and dry. If not, you will just have to do the best you can, cleaning them during the washing process.

Gently sprinkle the head and neck area with preservative. Take your scalpel and make a cut along the line formed where the skin meets feathers. Continue all the way around, staying as close as possible to the feather line. As soon as you possibly can, begin sprinkling preservative on the inside of the neck. This helps absorb the heavy fluids that are in the head and neck area. With the head free from the skin, either dispose of it, if an artificial is to be used, or prepare it for freeze-drying.

At this point you can continue with fleshing and degreasing or you can place the skin in the freezer to continue working on later. If you choose to store the skin, make certain that feathers won't be broken or crushed. I prefer to store a turkey skin in a small bag on top of any other items.

CHAPTER 5

Fleshing and Degreasing

I will never forget my first experience with a wild turkey. I awoke early that spring morning to the sound of raindrops spattering on the tent roof. Oh, great, I thought, there is nothing worse than hunting in the rain—other than having to work on a sunny spring day. Being the devoted hunter that I am, I headed afield. After unsuccessfully trying to gain the interest of an area gobbler, I decided to find a dry location to wait out the shower.

Once I found a semi-dry spot I began my wait. As I had gotten no response from nearby gobblers, I half-heartedly gave several lonely yelps. Still no response. As my mind began to drift, a movement on a nearby ridge caught my eye. With my attention focused on the movement, I noticed three birds ambling single file down the side of the ridge. One longbeard and two jakes made up the bachelor group. After many fruitless hunts in the mountains of North Carolina I knew I was moments away from becoming a successful turkey hunter.

Because I was eager to harvest a bird—my first bird—size didn't really matter. The best candidate would be the first one to come within range. A jake was the leader in line, and I steadily held the crosshairs on his vividly colored head. As the shot rang out the other birds made a hasty escape as their partner lay on the ground. I hurried to my prize. I was excited to say the least, but a question quickly came to mind.

Although it had been raining for some time, the bird I had harvested was almost completely dry. This made no sense to me as I had obtained a status somewhere between wet and completely drenched. It wasn't until I became involved in taxidermy that I learned why that bird was dry and I wasn't. Turkeys are very oily birds. This oil is present for good reason. It helps nearly all birds shed water. Otherwise, each time a rain came, the turkeys would be hard pressed to maintain their high temperatures. With lower than normal temperatures, their health could easily suffer. Also, wet feathers could hamper escape from predators, which wouldn't be good for the population.

These oils, although beneficial to the turkey while it is alive and well, can be detrimental to the work of the taxidermist trying to preserve this beautiful bird.

Through the years I have seen numerous turkey mounts. Some were good, some not so good. To the inexperienced eye, a poor job may simply be chalked up to poor mounting skills. But there may be more to the situation than that. Using the best techniques in the world will produce horrible results if the turkey skin isn't properly fleshed and degreased.

I learned this the hard way. My first turkey mount was nothing short of disastrous. After reading a book on how to mount birds, I was eager to get started. Once the job was finished, I knew something just wasn't right, despite the compliments I received. I obtained the telephone number for an experienced bird taxidermist and told him of my problem. On hearing about the dull-looking feathers that were sticking together, my knowledgeable friend knew the problem. "What did you degrease the bird with?" he asked. "Degrease?" I said. "What is degreasing?"

That was the problem, of course. I unhappily disassembled the bird, degreased, and remounted it. It turned out okay for a first attempt, but without the direction I received from an experienced taxidermist, that bird would have been stored away permanently to hide its terrible appearance.

All techniques must be executed properly to produce a quality mount, although some procedures will carry more weight than others. Fleshing and degreasing is one of those important steps that rank near the top of the list. If you cut a couple of holes during skinning you can sew them up. If you shift a feather tract slightly during the mounting, it will probably go unnoticed to all but a trained taxidermist. But mount a bird with flat, lifeless feathers and even a child will notice.

Fortunately, proper fleshing and degreasing are relatively simple procedures. As with the other steps, this isn't a race. Take your time and do it right. An experienced taxidermist may flesh a bird in less than 30 minutes, but it may take a novice more than an hour. Once everything is complete, you will be glad you spent the extra time to do it right.

Although we have already discussed tools, I'd like to again stress the need for quality equipment. The fleshing process will incorporate the use of scissors, snips, and a fleshing wheel, with the latter requiring the largest investment. For those who aren't sure if turkey taxidermy is something they want to continue, there may be some hesitation about spending a large sum of money for tools. Rest assured, though, whether your stay in the field of taxidermy is short or lasts a lifetime you will never regret purchasing quality equipment. When I started out I thought I could get by without a fleshing wheel. I quickly found this piece of equipment invaluable.

By doing the math it is easy to understand you are getting a bargain with even the best tools. Most fan mounts will cost the hunter an average of $75, breast mounts start around $250, and a life-sized mount will cost anywhere between $400 and $800, depending on where you live. You could easily get by with spending around $200 for your own equipment, but if you spend $400 this investment will easily pay for itself, even if you only complete three fan mounts. If you are like many of the outdoorsmen I know, however, you will quickly become addicted to wildlife artistry. And once the addiction sets in, three fan mounts will be a drop in the bucket.

There are a few things you need to understand in order to begin proper fleshing. One is that clean feathers with properly fleshed roots are much easier to work with. A good gauge for whether or not your fleshing has been properly done is feather position. Once the turkey is dry, feather position should change very little from when it was first mounted. In poorly fleshed skins, the tissue surrounding the feather quills will shrink and shift as it dries. As this tissue shifts, so do the feathers. So it is important that each feather base is relatively clean.

FLESHING

Before starting you must completely invert the turkey skin. To do this, simply reach inside through the incision already made. Grasp the neck area and pull through this incision. Be careful not to tear

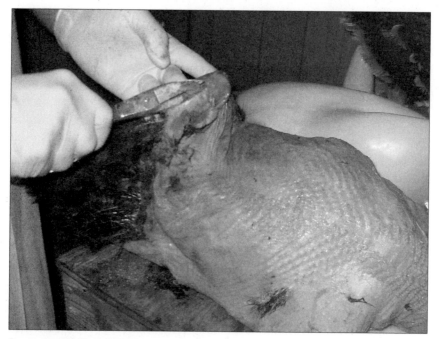

Removing flesh with scissors.

anything. Now, completely invert the legs and the wings as far as they will go, and you are ready to continue.

The fat content of turkeys will vary. Food availability, along with a particular bird's eagerness to breed, will affect how fat a bird happens to be. Most birds in the early spring season will at least have a thick sponge of fat in the breast area, and this is probably the toughest area to clean properly.

Getting this flesh free from the skin usually begins with a pair of scissors or snips. I have learned that by sprinkling the fatty tissue with a preservative the slippery tissue can be more easily gripped and pulled free. I will even pinch up certain areas with my fingers, pulling the excess flesh free. But be careful doing this. Early in my career I grabbed hold of some muscle and fat tissue and began to pull. When I did I pulled several feathers completely through the skin. From then on I was very cautious about ripping any tissue from the skin. When in doubt, use scissors. Also, try to avoid cutting any feather roots with the scissors; this too will cause unwanted feather loss.

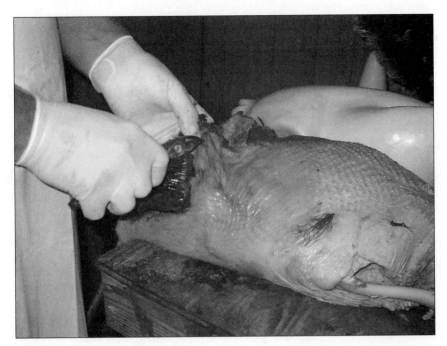

Removing flesh with snips.

Another great tool to use during the initial fat removal is a pair of cutting pliers or snips. In particularly tough areas these pliers can be used to snip away or grasp the fat area and pull it free.

After the bulk of the fat is pulled free, it is time to turn your attention to the fleshing wheel. The wheel I use is a Van Dyke Bird Flesher manufactured by Van Dyke's Taxidermy Supply. I mention this particular brand because it has earned a good reputation and is reasonably priced in comparison to similar fleshers. No matter what type you choose, be sure to obtain one with a large enough motor to wheel away stubborn turkey fat yet small enough to stop turning should the turkey skin be jerked from your hands and wrapped around the brush. A good average motor is ¼ horsepower. Don't let getting the skin wrapped around the brush scare you, because it is going to happen. It happens to the best in the industry. You just need to be sure that your fleshing motor is small enough that it won't continue after becoming entangled.

By using a systematic method, I can flesh a bird more thoroughly and quickly. It is best to start on the front of the bird and

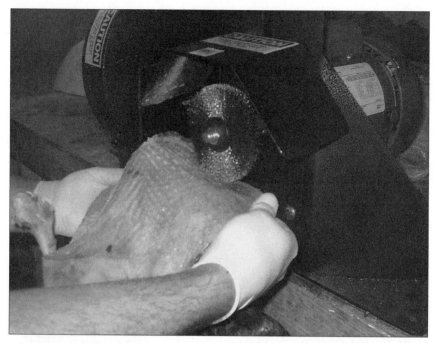

A Van Dyke's flesher in use.

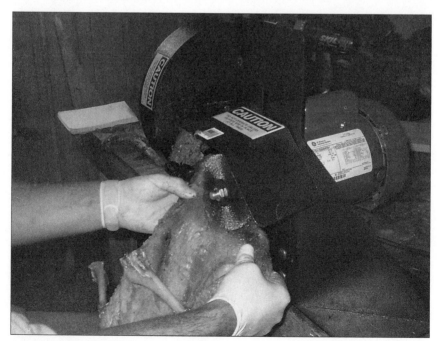

Using the Van Dyke's flesher on the skin.

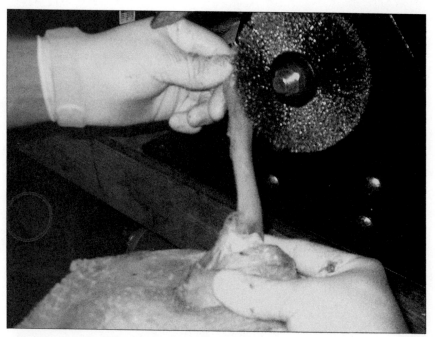

Use of a flesher to clean any bones is beneficial.

work your way back. Moving from left to right as the brush turns clockwise is ideal. This throws the flesh onto the trail of the wire brush rather than into its path. If you work in the opposite direction you will eventually build up a large amount of fat in front of the working brush. (Much like a snowplow accumulates snow in front of the blade.) Eventually, there will be too much to push. This slows progress and could cause burning or tears.

You will quickly find out that a turkey isn't made up of a mass of feathers. Instead, there are several different feather tracts. It is best to work on these feather tracts separately. I begin fleshing the wing bones, then the leg bones, then continue on to the skin. Usually, I begin with the breast section because this area will probably be the toughest to flesh thoroughly, and I want to be fresh while doing this work. Depending on the particular bird, I have found the other tracts much easier to flesh. I then continue with the back, scapulars, and thigh area. (Proper tail fleshing is detailed in chapter 7, Fan and Cape Preparation.)

Fleshing the leg bone.

When you are holding the inverted skin in your hands a pattern to the feather quills quickly becomes apparent. It looks somewhat like a cornfield, with all the quills arranged in rows. This actually makes it easier to perform the fleshing process. In the neck area, the feathers are very close together so I lightly go across the top, wheeling away the bulk of the flesh. Be careful in this tender area, holes are easily torn or burned. When you begin fleshing the body these rows will become wider and you will be able to place the wheel between each one. After all rows in a particular feather tract are clean, I turn the skin 90 degrees and continue wheeling away fat.

As you learn to use the fleshing wheel, you may find it helpful to keep a bucket of water nearby. You can occasionally dip the skin if it begins to get too hot. This heat is due to the friction of the wire wheel. Using a wheel may seem overwhelming at first, but you should quickly get a good feel for how much pressure is required to remove the unwanted flesh. After doing a thorough job with the

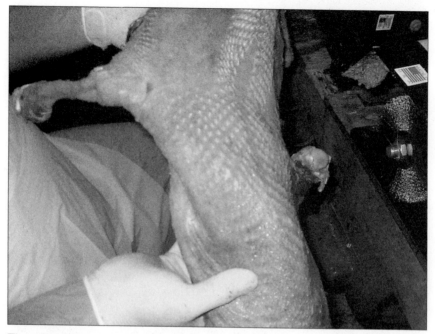

The pattern that should appear after proper fleshing.

fleshing machine you will probably need to shift back to the scissors. The scissors can be used to cut free any flesh that you weren't able to get with the wheel.

WASHING AND DEGREASING

With most of the visible fat and flesh removed, it is time to turn your attention to degreasing. A proper degreasing solution will yield beautiful oil-free feathers. Properly cleaned feathers have a shine matched only by those of a live, well-groomed bird.

Many methods exist for degreasing, but they all don't work equally well. Degreasing should begin with a bath, which eliminates excess blood, dirt, and other unwanted extras. An old standby for many years has been Dawn dishwashing liquid. Fill a large tub with cool water and squeeze in a small amount of Dawn. Make certain the detergent mixes well with the water. Don't worry about using too much because you will shortly rinse the excess.

Now submerge the turkey skin in the solution. Gently feel the wet feathers with your hands. You are feeling for any clumps of blood or dirt that may be stuck to the feathers. If you feel something unusual, gently work it free. A small toothbrush also works great when you are trying to clean the wing feathers. Brush gently with the grain of the feather until the stain is removed. I then grasp the wings and lightly work the skin with a back-and-forth, up-and-down motion. This should help loosen any unwanted particles that remain. At this point, I just let the skin soak for about an hour, depending on how dirty it is. If at all possible I will leave the tail section out of the bath. The tail is usually almost completely clean when the bird arrives so washing simply creates more work. (For complete care instructions for the tail refer to chapter 7, Fan and Cape Preparation.)

After at least an hour has elapsed I pull the skin from the bath by the wings. Grabbing any other area may cause the skin to tear. Once the skin is removed, thoroughly rinse the bird with water. The easiest approach is to either hang the bird or have someone hold it

An appropriate-sized bucket will be beneficial to degreasing. Many taxidermists value Dawn liquid as a washing and degreasing agent.

Immerse the skin into the washing solution.

Gently washing the feathers will remove most blood and dirt.

while you use a continually running water source to completely rinse. When the water running off is clear, the bird is rinsed thoroughly enough.

Some respected taxidermists believe that a bath in Dawn is all that is required to properly degrease even the oiliest skins. However, I like to continue the cleaning process with products made specifically for degreasing. There are several on the market, and I am not partial to any particular brand. With your degreaser of choice, mix up a large enough volume to again submerge the turkey skin. Then let it soak for at least 30 minutes. When working with a commercial degreaser, be sure to wear a pair of rubber gloves. Commercial degreasers are designed to remove oil so if you submerge your hands into a degreasing solution you will end up with severely dry skin, if not severe skin irritation.

You may eventually hear of a method that many bird taxidermists swear by for degreasing—a gas bath, using Coleman fuel or regular gasoline. I believe this method can be very dangerous, so I avoid it completely. Aside from being harmful to your health, I have heard horror stories of fires caused by the fumes. Although the initial cost is higher, specially made degreasers should be used instead; unless you decide, as many have, that just using Dawn is enough.

After I retrieve the skin from the degreaser, I once again rinse thoroughly and then let the skin drain for a few minutes. The next step may cause you trouble with your spouse, particularly if she is still wondering about your decision to mount your own trophy. Once the skin has drained for several minutes, I fold it wing to wing and place it into a washing machine. If the probability of causing too much domestic trouble is high, it may be best to purchase a used washer for your shop. You should be able to find a cheap one, because all that you need it to do is spin. Set the machine for a long spin and let it do its thing.

Upon removal, the skin should be more damp than wet. To complete the drying of the feathers, you can hang the skin overnight or begin drying immediately.

I usually begin by laying the bird on a dry towel. (The dry towel will help pull out some of the moisture.) I then use a hair dryer to finish the drying process. I like a dryer that allows me to turn off the heat element if I choose to. Initially, the heat will be left on, but as

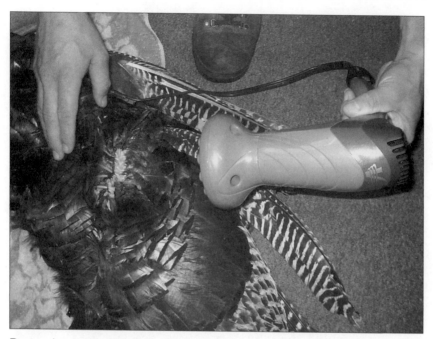

Drying thoroughly before any work begins is very important.

the feathers dry I may cut it to avoid overheating the skin. I generally concentrate my initial efforts with the dryer on the neck feathers. These are so fragile I like to get the inside of the skin dry, as well as the outside feathers, before continuing with the rest of the bird.

Once the feathers are almost completely dry, I tumble the turkey for less than a minute in a mixture of corncob grit and preservative. This helps remove any moisture that may be left in the feathers. If you don't have a tumbler, continue using the dryer until you are confident that all feathers are completely dry. Occasionally, I will hold the turkey by its wings and gently shake it during the drying process. This helps the feathers fall into place.

When you complete the fleshing and degreasing process you should be left with a turkey skin with no residue. As stated earlier, the quality of the job you do here will be evident long after the mounting process is finished, so take the time to do it well.

CHAPTER 6

Preservation Methods

A fter the skinning, fleshing, degreasing, and drying are complete it is time to preserve the skin. Preserving the skin allows you to enjoy your work of art for as long as possible—hopefully a lifetime. And this even applies to your first mount. As your work progresses, and I can assure you that it will if you devote time to the art, you will still enjoy looking back on your first few attempts. You'll not only appreciate the trophy you collected, but the improvements you have made during the learning process. Because you will want all your creations to last, you should properly utilize the best preservation methods available. Ultimately, only you can make the decision about which methods and products suit you.

If your stay in taxidermy is longer than a couple of minutes you will no doubt be sucked into the controversy surrounding preservation methods. Debate over dry preservative versus a true tan has raged for years.

Advocates of dry preservative believe it is quick and reliable. They also think a great finished product can be achieved. Many world-class taxidermists use only a dry preservative, and they earn blue ribbons, as well as respect, in national and world competitions.

Other experts competing right beside these dry preservative advocates swear by a tanned product. Those who use only tanning methods are fewer in number, but they insist tanning is a much more effective method of preservation with a longer product life and that it is easier to work with. Complete tanning involves a full list of steps that include salting through the final tanning soak. There are also modern-day methods that simply involve a soak in a tanning solution. You will quickly find that methods vary and that most hobbyists and full-timers have a preferred approach.

To help you form your own opinion, we'll look at the particulars of each method.

Dry Preservative

So what exactly is dry preservative and what does it do? Dry preservative is a powdered chemical substance that, if applied properly, will preserve and protect the skin from bacteria growth. Most dry preservatives are a mix of chemicals that include ingredients that discourage bugs from infesting the specimen as well as help eliminate odors. Moths can be especially detrimental to a mount. So the bug deterrent is a definite advantage for the dry preservative. But many taxidermists claim that this bug proofing will eventually dissipate, leaving the trophy vulnerable to infestation. I have not had any problems with bugs, nor have the experienced taxidermists I know. As with any organic product, if the conditions are ideal bug problems may sooner or later be encountered. To avoid damage one must regularly monitor the mount and act accordingly. Although many taxidermists call any powdered method a "quick tan," no stabilization of the structural proteins within the skin actually takes place when using dry preservative. So its use shouldn't be considered a tan.

Dry preserved skins of any kind, mammal or bird, are essentially rawhide with the moisture removed. They can return to a raw state at any time, should enough moisture contaminate the skin. But the moisture content in the air would have to be extremely high for a very long time to return a dry preserved skin to a raw state. The same moisture level could have a harmful effect on tanned skins as well, although it would not return a tanned skin to rawhide.

Because skin is made up of approximately 60 to 70 percent moisture, it can easily be destroyed by bacteria if left untreated. To help eliminate moisture in the skin, dry preservative is heavily composed of desiccants. Desiccants are chemical drying agents that absorb and help prevent the recurrence of moisture in the skin. This is how dry preservative got its name: It preserves through a drying action. And because bacteria, which breaks down the skin, can't exist in a moisture-free environment, no deterioration takes place. The desiccant-laden dry preservative effectively preserves the skin by keeping it dry.

A second major ingredient of dry preservative is a surfactant. Surfactants are used to aid the absorption of the desiccant, allowing it to do its job. Scientifically speaking, the surfactant lowers the surface tension of the moisture in the skin. This counters the raw skin's natural tendency to repel foreign substances, increasing penetration.

There are some things you can do to help alleviate any problems associated with the dry preservative method. One is to allow whatever dry preservative you use to penetrate the skin thoroughly. It is sometimes best to heavily apply the preservative, then fold up the skin and lay it on a towel in a refrigerated or cool area. Let it stay there overnight before shaking the excess free and reapplying.

Once the mount is completed, keep it in a controlled environment. Ideal conditions are between 60 and 80 degrees with low humidity, which holds true for tanned products as well.

When using dry preservative a major key to quality is the removal of all fats, muscle tissues, and membranes. This may be the single most important factor, as excessive fats or tissues, if left attached, can cause excessive shrinkage. The removal of excess tissues is also a factor in the tanning process, but it is more relevant to dry preserving.

Because more shrinkage will occur with the dry preservative process, numerous pins should be used to keep the overall mount from shifting major feather tracts as it dries. Some taxidermists like to apply a generous hide paste, but in my opinion this will cause more problems than it is worth. I just use plenty of pins. If you choose to use hide paste, be careful with it because it is very difficult to remove from the feathers should a mishap occur.

TANNING

Understanding the chemical composition changes that take place within a skin during the tanning process should help you decide whether to choose this method. Those who decide on the tanning system usually do so because they believe that the skin is stable and that less shrinkage will occur.

To understand this stability you must first know of what skin is actually comprised. Skin is a mix of moisture and proteins, but within the group of proteins there are soluble and insoluble proteins. I once read a very accurate description of skin composition in a "breakthrough" taxidermy manual. The manual stated that a good analogy for skin would be to think of a skin as a leafy tree. The trunk and limbs can be considered the structural, or insoluble, proteins. The leaves represent the blood, fats, and soluble proteins. To stabilize a skin you must first remove these leaves, so that only the leafless limbs remain. But you can't stop at this stage or your tree limbs will eventually collapse because nothing is cushioning the limb's surroundings. Basically, this means that when dry preservative is used a bulk of the soluble proteins are pulled from the skin, but they are replaced with nothing. This is why a bit more shrinkage occurs in a dry preserved skin. When tanning is completed properly the leaves, or soluble proteins, are replaced with tannins. Tannins can be thought of as artificial leaves, acting as fillers that attach to the skeletal, or insoluble, structure. These tannins will also help lubricate the structure, preventing it from eventually collapsing and becoming glued together. At least in theory, this leaves you with less shrinkage and a more stable final product.

The complete tanning process can include up to three steps, which are preceded by salting, degreasing, and washing. Very few taxidermists use the lengthy method of conventional tanning for birds; however, it might be beneficial to the beginner to understand all the processes that are available beyond dry preservative. Another advantage of knowing the tanning process is that the steps are nearly the same for mammals. This is helpful to know if you decide to continue learning more about taxidermy.

If you choose to conventionally tan a skin you will begin by applying a layer of salt after the skin has been properly fleshed. This extracts the soluble proteins—blood, fats, and oils—from the skin. Although it may take several days to remove these unwanted items when salting mammals, only a couple of hours are necessary when salt is applied to a bird skin, primarily because a bird skin is very thin.

Once the salt has done its job you will continue to degrease and wash the skin. First, shake the excess salt from the skin. When degreasing, your goal is to remove any fats and oils that remain. This will give the feathers a luster that would otherwise be dulled from the oils. After a soak of 20 minutes to an hour, remove the skin. The length of time in the degreaser depends on how oily the skin is judged to be. After removal from a degreaser, the skin should be thoroughly washed and rinsed. Washing and degreasing is covered thoroughly in chapter 5.

Continue the process by placing the skin into a salt solution with a ratio of 1½ cups of salt to 1 gallon of cold water. Soak the skin for approximately 30 minutes. This salt solution is important because it will prevent the skin from acid swelling from the pickle solution used in the next step.

Now place the skin into a pickle bath, which is a mixture of salt and acid. (The best acids for bird skin include citric acid as well as pickling crystals that have been specifically formulated for bird skins. These can be obtained from most taxidermy suppliers). A pickle bath is used to further dissolve and remove the soluble proteins within the skin. The acid will also break up the natural bonds of the proteins and prepare the skin fibers to bond with the tannins that will be introduced in the tanning bath. For birds, it is important that you use a mild acid. After mixing the pickle, check the pH. Ideally, the pH should be between 4.5 and 5. (Most acid comes with instructions on how to achieve the proper pH levels.) Soak the skin in this pickle bath for 45 minutes to an hour. At this point the skin is ready to place into the tan.

The process of soaking the turkey in a bird tan will replace the previously removed soluble proteins with tannins. This is important because if you don't introduce the tannins you might as well have skipped the previous steps. As with the pickle, several bird tans are available. Initially, it is a simple matter of trial and error or talking to on-staff taxidermists like those employed by Van Dykes Taxidermy Supply. After soaking for about an hour the skin is ready to remove. When drying is complete the mounting process may continue.

Taxidermists have used dry preservative for many years, but technology has also shown us newer ways to preserve skin. After sifting through this array of information you may become overwhelmed. Don't be. After many years in the taxidermy business I have formed the opinion that nothing is always right and nothing is always wrong.

Advancements come from those willing to try things that no one else will. The bottom line is that if it suits you give it a try. I base a lot of what I choose on the current circumstances. Customers that want things done a certain way and how well the bird or animal has been cared for each play a major role in my decision-making process. As you progress, you will begin forming your own opinions. Whatever method you choose, do it well and you will reach your goal.

Throughout this book we will refer to the dry preservative method because it is an excellent way for the beginner to get started. Dry preservative is very easy to apply, and I feel it is 100 percent effective. As your skills grow, you may choose to switch to the tanning method.

CHAPTER 7

Fan and Cape Preparation

M ost people who attempt the art of turkey taxidermy will eventually mount a full bird, but an excellent way to get your feet wet is to mount a couple of fans or maybe a cape. These are relatively easy and will provide a solid foundation of knowledge and experience that you can build on. Fan preparation may seem to need no explanation, but this is far from the truth.

I have had clients or friends over the years that have requested that I take a look at their handiwork. Their half-hearted attempt usually resulted in a fan base full of meat and fat (this is an excellent way to produce happy and healthy bugs). Once, after being told by a client that he had removed every last bit of meat, I was able to cut away slightly more than a golf-ball-sized amount. The hunter was astounded.

Fans that are improperly cleaned will usually look okay at first, but after the drying process the feather tips will become uneven and wavy. This is a result of the meat drying at different speeds, which in turn pulls quills in different directions and into different shapes.

The tools needed to complete the fan mount are a scalpel, dry preservative, needle-nose pliers, scissors, a flat clean surface large enough to accommodate a spread fan, and a small amount of bondo (which is optional).

Before you get started make sure your work area is clean and that your hands remain clean while touching any feathers. It is easy to start with clean hands, but once any incisions are made, grease from fat and muscle tissue will sometimes taint your hands, eventually ending up on the feathers. If this happens, quickly wipe your hands free of grease or change gloves; gloves should be worn during all taxidermy procedures. It is always easier to maintain clean feathers than to try to clean them later.

SEPARATING THE TAIL FROM THE CARCASS

To free the tail from the body, grasp the tail with one hand and make a perpendicular cut at the base of the tail, across the anal opening. Cut all the way through the end of the spine. Go slowly, being careful not to inadvertently cut the skin free from the back in the wrong place. If you do happen to cut through in an undesired location simply reattach the section. Once the base of the spine is severed, look at the back of the bird. For a fan, you should keep the secondary feathers, which are the next longest to the primaries, and a half-dozen rows of back feathers attached to the tail. If you end up with a few more, this is fine. Any excess may be trimmed at a later time.

SKINNING AND CLEANING THE FEATHER BASES

After the tail is free from the carcass the more tedious work begins. Lay the tail section in a clean area. Then begin separating the skin from the muscle tissue with a fresh scalpel. Free the skin almost the entire way to where the quills enter the body, stopping short by only about ⅛ inch. If you try to go much farther, cutting through the skin may be unavoidable. The skin in this area is very tender so try to cut more toward the muscle tissue while skinning. Skinning all the way back should reveal the upper base of the quills.

If the skin is pulled back far enough you will find the oil glands. The oil glands are located just under the back skin and appear as two small, rounded, fatty tissues that are full of yellow oil. These glands must be taken out to avoid further oil bleeding. To remove the glands without damaging the back skin, use a pair of scissors or a scalpel to cut cautiously until the glands are free. After the glands are removed, inspect the small portion of back skin. Remove any flesh that remains. Sprinkling dry preservative on the skin will make the flesh easier to grasp and pull free from the skin.

At this point, use the scalpel to cut a short V in the center of the quills. The tail section, or tip of the spine, still remains in the center

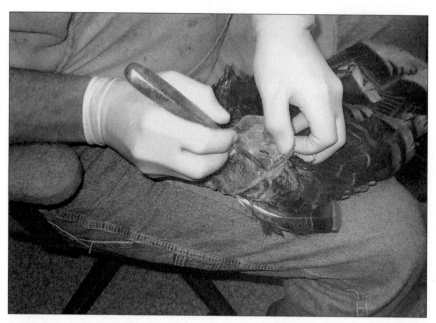

Freeing the skin from the muscle tissue should always be done very cautiously to avoid cutting the skin.

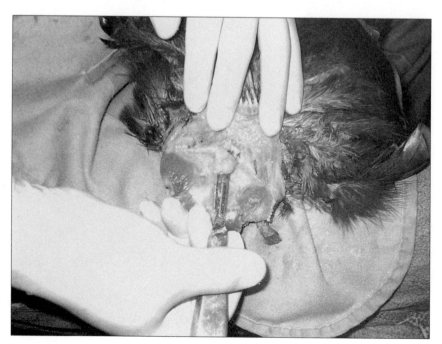

Removing the oil gland in base of tail.

of the quills; it can be removed before or after the muscle tissue. It is sometimes easier to remove this piece of bone before the process of fleshing because if the tip is left intact it may cause your knife to hang while trying to make the necessary cuts. Once the proper V-cut is made, and after pushing the tip into the center of the tail, use needle-nose pliers to grasp the tail section and give a strong tug. It may take several attempts to remove. If the tail section breaks off while you are trying to remove it, reach in a bit farther, grasp the broken tip, and try again. If for some reason you are unable to remove this small bone it isn't a major concern, but it is preferable, as it will make the feathers much easier to place when the time comes to spread them in position.

Now take the scalpel and cautiously cut from where the skin attaches to the feathers to the quill tips. This cut should be made parallel to the quills and as close as possible. Your goal is to free the quills of any muscle tissue on both the front and back. The quills are very tender and are easily cut with a scalpel.

It is very important to remove as much tissue and fat as possible. After successfully cutting free the bulk of the tissue on the front

Cutting between each quill will aid in fat removal.

Fleshing the feather quills.

and back, you will notice a small bit of fat between each quill. This is removed by making small cuts between each quill. Subsequent to making these cuts, grasp the quill near the base and use a small pair of wire cutters to firmly tug until the fat is removed from each individual quill. Upon completion, the quills should be free of one another. Now use a quality bird flesher on the quills. To do this, pull the skin back and gently clean each side of the tail base with the wire wheel; this will aid in the final fat removal.

Once all fat is removed from the quills, generously dust the exposed quills and skin with a dry preservative. Then spread the fan and check for any dirt, grease, or blood. If proper care has been taken during the skinning process and the bird was properly cared for in the field the fan should have very little, if any, of these contaminants. If the feathers are clean and in good condition, move on to mounting the fan.

If the fan is in poor shape due to dirty or deformed feathers, a thorough washing is in order. The most efficient method for cleaning feathers is with a degreaser. Many taxidermists use a small amount of Dawn dishwashing liquid in water. I prefer a stronger degreaser like those found at Van Dykes Taxidermy Supply. After a solution is mixed, soak the fan for approximately 15 minutes to allow the degreaser to do its job. Then remove the fan and make sure it is rinsed thoroughly. Soap residue left on the feathers will reduce quality, so keep rinsing until the water is completely clear. After a thorough washing and drying, reapply the dry preservative.

If the feathers have been bent from improper storage or handling a short soak in hot water should straighten them. If a feather is broken or missing you can pull it out and replace with a matching tail feather of good quality. If only one feather is bad and you are not able to obtain another, simply close up the gap with the remaining feathers.

MOUNTING THE FAN

The fan is now ready for mounting, and two different methods can be used. For one, the fan can simply be opened to a desirable posi-

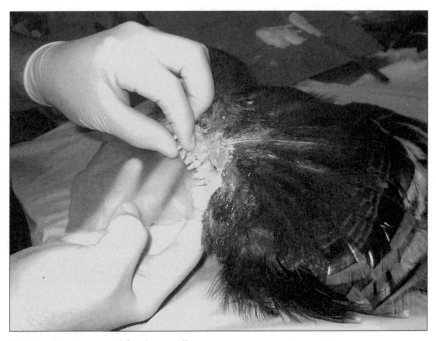

Placing plastic around feather quills.

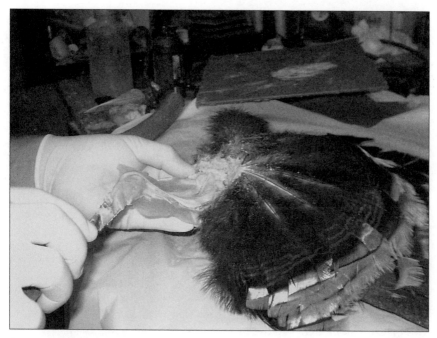

Placing bondo in plastic.

tion and secured to a flat surface. The drying time will depend on temperature and humidity. I normally leave it alone for at least two weeks. After the two-week period, free the fan from the surface. If the feathers are rigid and stay open, the fan should be dry enough to continue mounting to a plaque. If you are mounting a life-sized bird, set the fan aside until it is needed.

The second method of positioning a tail—and the one I prefer—involves the addition of a golf-ball-sized portion of bondo. With this method, the fan is open and ready for placement on a plaque or for mounting in less than 30 minutes.

To apply bondo, spread the fan on a flat surface. Then lay a piece of plastic under the quills and wrap it over the front of them. Mix the bondo, then lift the top of the plastic and spread a small portion under and over the exposed quills. Lay the plastic back over the top and press lightly, making sure the bondo is worked between each quill. Try to avoid using an excessive amount, as this may cause problems when you attach the fan to a form or plaque. If

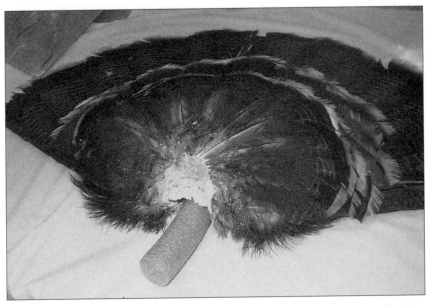

When preparing the fan for a strutting or flying mount, it will be beneficial to give the fan a slight arch—do this by placing a small item under the quills.

Once the bondo is applied, quickly reposition the fan.

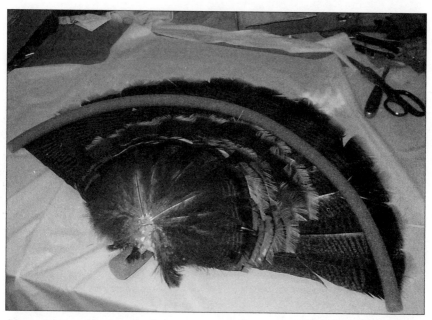

Also, when positioning the fan, it is wise to lay a small weight on the feathers which will help them maintain their position.

you make a mistake, the bondo can easily be removed after it begins to harden. You'll be able to try again without harm to the fan.

CAPE PREPARATION

Once a turkey hunter possesses several fans, he may next want to preserve a cape. This amounts to a fan with the entire back skin attached. These are beautiful, and I find them more aesthetically appealing than a simple fan.

As discussed earlier, turkeys have several different feather tracts instead of just a mass of random feathers. For the caping procedure, locate the feather tract along the top of the back that extends from head to tail. Use a knife to cut along each side of the feather tract from where the tail meets the body to the neck, where the feathers meet the skin. Detach the tail on the underside the same way you would for a fan, leaving it attached to the back skin. Sever the skin at a position near the head area, then skin it until it is free from the body. To avoid moisture from saturating the cape as it is skinned,

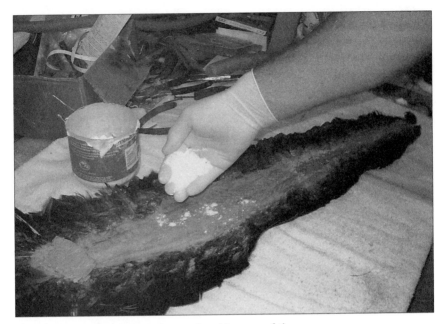

Generously apply preservative to the skin area of the cape.

generously apply preservative to the skin and carcass as it is pulled free. Applying dry preservative to the skin side also makes flesh removal from the skin easier. Fleshing the back skin can be done by hand or with a flesher, but make sure there are no large amounts of flesh left attached. Depending on the cleanliness of the feathers, you may choose to continue with the positioning process or you may need to wash the cape.

Once you are ready to proceed, generously dust the skin and fan with a dry preservative. To prepare the cape for drying you can either place both the fan and cape on a flat, clean surface, spreading each to its desired position, or you can bondo the tail then attach it and the back skin to a flat surface.

Once again, I prefer the bondo method. The fan usually takes the longest to dry, but the skin can dry in only a few days. If the fan is secured with bondo you have a finished product in less than half the time.

After completing either the cape or fan, the aspiring taxidermist may wish to add the beard and preserved feet and wings. These

Prepared cape.

extra touches enhance an already beautiful addition to any trophy room.

Fans or capes are excellent for hunters with limited space or for those without the time to invest in a life-sized mount. Whatever your choice, it will be an excellent memento of a past hunt. Fans and capes also make excellent gifts for hunting buddies or family members who enjoy the outdoors.

CHAPTER 8

A Breast Mount

A n excellent intermediate project for anyone learning turkey taxidermy is the breast mount. Good experience may be gained by completing this project. Because a breast mount doesn't normally include the wings or legs, wiring isn't required and body posture isn't a factor, but valuable knowledge will be gained through skinning, fleshing, and degreasing. Also, head and fan attachment are required, so you are basically crafting a mini version

of a life-sized mount. This experience will pay huge dividends when you tackle bigger projects.

Another advantage is that a breast mount can be extended to include the wings or the legs. While the wings would have to be properly fleshed and wired, the legs require nothing more than the injection of preservative, painting, and attachment to a panel.

For those who are practicing taxidermy for the first time I would recommend skinning the bird for a life-sized mount. This will give you experience in the skinning department and will ensure that the cape for the breast mount isn't cut too short. When skinning for a breast, or half mount as it is sometimes called, leave the tail attached to the skin until the bird is completely skinned.

After skinning is complete and before the fleshing takes place, slip the breast manikin into the skin. Position the skin correctly, and use the scalpel to trim off the excess. To make sure that enough skin is available, cut the skin at least 2 inches longer than needed. You can always come back later and trim the overhang. It will probably be easiest to trim the skin from the underside. This will eliminate cutting any important feathers.

Now cut the tail free from the remaining body skin. Be sure to include several rows of back feathers. This will help with blending the back feathers on the cape into the tail. The feathers on the underside of the tail aren't as important. You may even choose to cut free the skin that is located on the underside of the tail, although I would leave it attached through the bondo process, in which the tail is permanently positioned. This will help with positioning when it is time to attach the tail between the breast and the panel. Continue spreading and positioning the fan, using the bondo method.

After your cape is cut to the desired length and the tail is cut free it is time to continue with proper fleshing and degreasing. Once again, the short cape provides a great learning experience, even for the prep work. The tasks are the same, but you will be working for shorter lengths of time with a lighter, smaller skin, which will allow you to concentrate better on the detail work.

Use the same methods described in chapter 5, Fleshing and Degreasing, to prepare the cape for mounting. Go the extra mile to eliminate as much fat as possible on the breast, as this area can be a trouble spot. After completing the prep work and properly drying the feathers of the cape, you are ready to continue.

The supplies necessary to complete this project include a turkey breast manikin, the head of your choice, a completed fan, and a

panel suitable for the breast mount. (These supplies will be in addition to your other taxidermy tools.) Panels and their prices vary
greatly. Some panels are touted as being specifically for breast
mounts, but I have attached most of my breast mounts to shoulder
mount panels. A 16- by 20-inch panel is ideal. These are less expensive and have a greater variety of shapes.

You should have already applied dry preservative on the cape,
but to ensure saturation shake loose any excess, then reapply. Now
slide the cape onto the manikin. The neck on the manikin should
be inserted through the neck of the cape. Once the cape is in place
pin the beard just below where the neck and breast join. This is an
excellent reference point. After its attachment, the skin should virtually fall into a correct anatomical position. Only fine adjustments
should be needed to obtain a finished product.

If there is excess skin on the back simply slide it forward toward
the back of the neck. This extra skin will give the full, fluffy look
that should be your goal. If the excess skin appears unnatural you
may have to trim a small portion, but do so sparingly.

Before permanently attaching the skin to the manikin, attach the
manikin to the center of the chosen panel using three 1½- to 2-inch
screws. Pre-drill three holes to what will be the attachment point of
the breast manikin. This point can be found easily by placing the
manikin onto the middle of the panel. This position will be very
close to perfect, and final adjustments may be made later.

After the attachment has been made, gradually begin trimming
the cape to better fit the manikin. Then start lightly pulling the
feathers forward with a regulator needle. This will give the breast a
full appearance. Pulling the feathers forward will also show you
which feathers are excessive. For best results, trim only one row of
feathers at a time. Each time a row is eliminated fluff the breast to
determine whether more should be removed. You may need to remove the skin past the manikin back. This is fine, as the feathers
will easily hide the light colored manikin. Also, the breast will join
the panel better without a bulky excess layer of skin between the
two.

Three reference points are available to ensure the skin is in the
proper position before you continue. The beard, which you should
have temporarily attached, is one. The other two are the center of
the breast and the center of the back. When you are sure the cape is
in position begin pinning the skin. The skin should be pinned at the
edge in 1½-inch intervals.

When all the pins are in place it is time to attach the tail. Some taxidermists choose to attach the tail before positioning the skin, but I find it easier to position the skin then slide the tail into its pre-slotted location. To attach the tail, loosen the three screws used to secure the manikin to the panel. Don't remove the screws, though, as this will only cause more problems when it comes time to re-attach them. With the screws loosened, slide the tail down into the tail slot.

If the bondo portion at the base of the tail feathers is too thick you may need to use a dremel tool to grind down the width. Once the tail slides easily into place, moderately tighten the screws. After evenly situating the tail section and readjusting the breast and back feathers, finish tightening the screws. If the tail section is too loose you may have to place two more screws through the bondo portion of the tail. This should firmly anchor the fan. Now you will be ready to attach a pre-painted head.

Most turkey breast manikins come with necks already attached. These necks are usually made of the same foam as the manikin. This foam isn't flexible so it is best to remove it and replace it with soft flexible neck material in the 1- to 1¼-inch range. To do this, simply cut the hard neck at the base. Leave the pre-attached wire, and slide on the new neck material. A flexible neck is important when positioning the head, but be sure not to use an excessively long neck. The head should be pulled to the rear and downward, just as a live bird would do while strutting.

If you choose to go ahead and add wings, cut them free from the body skin just above the shoulder area. Specially-made panels should be used when attaching the wings. These panels are elongated and visible between the two outstretched wings. Begin by properly prepping the wings. (Wing preparation is detailed in chapter 9, Pre-Mounting Procedures.) Then attach the wings to the panel alongside the breast mount. The wings will hang vertically along the narrow panel.

In addition to being a great learning experience, the breast mount is perfect for hunters with limited space for a mount. It can be hung on the wall out of the way of children or pets. Also, the breast mount can be completed in a relatively short amount of time. While it is often overlooked as an option for preserving trophies, you will quickly find it a great addition to your own collection, particularly if you already have all the other poses.

CHAPTER 9

Pre-Mounting Procedures

Before reaching this point you should have completed plenty of research and preparation. Your preparation can be compared to gathering parts of a puzzle. To finish, you must put all the pieces together. In my opinion, if everything from field care through degreasing has been done properly, the mounting will be the easy part. When deciding which pose to tackle first, it is usually best to start slowly. As you gain experience you will be able to complete all the turkey poses you desire.

The breast mount would have to be considered the easiest mount; next in line would be the flying bird. It is often said that a taxidermist has made a significant accomplishment if he or she earns a blue ribbon at a taxidermy competition with a strutting bird. There is no doubt that the strutting pose is one of the toughest mounts to pull off, but a simple closed-wing standing bird is also one of the most difficult to mount accurately. The reason a standing bird is so tough is that if the anatomy isn't almost perfect the entire mount will look out of proportion. This is also true with any of the other poses, of course, but there is a bit more room for error with the others. With this in mind, it is usually best to start out with either the breast mount or flying mount.

Most life-sized turkey poses begin almost identically. Each bird, no matter the chosen pose, must be preserved and wired, and a bit more fleshing must be done to the wing area. The difference between poses is mainly what size wire goes into the wings or legs. Obviously, the heads will differ, as will the final pose, but nearly all of the initial techniques will be the same.

Before continuing, make certain your work area is clean. You've put lots of effort into maintaining the cleanliness of the feathers, and it is important to strive for this same cleanliness throughout the

71

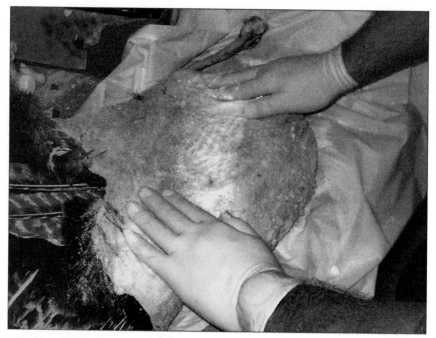

We have chosen the dry preserved method.

mounting process. Cover your worktable with freezer paper or permanently attach a piece of wallpaper or something similar. The main objective is to maintain a surface that doesn't readily hold dirt or debris. Also, a snag-free surface that won't damage feathers is important. Be sure to wipe the surface clean after each step.

You should also start with a dry bird. Dry feathers will add loft and be much easier to work with and position. I like to use a hair dryer to fluff the feathers immediately prior to the mounting process. Not only do the feathers need to be completely dry, so does the down underneath. This is actually what gives the full look to the feathers as they lay on the body. Without dry down, the feathers would look flat and lifeless. After the mount is complete, use a hair dryer once again to add body to the turkey. With all the handling the turkey receives throughout the mounting process some of the feathers may have gotten moist from the skin or mashed flat. This blowing action will once again provide fullness and add life.

Removing wing meat.

With your work area clean and all the necessary tools at hand, you are ready to start. Begin by laying the turkey on its back with the underside of the wings exposed. Because you only skinned the wings to the humerus-radius-ulna joint, you will now have to remove the meat in the last two sections. The reason you don't remove these muscles in the skinning process is that water could enter the quills of the wing feathers during the washing stage. This would eventually sour, causing a bad odor and possibly even mold.

To remove this tissue, cut lengthwise along the radius-ulna bones with a scalpel. This cut should be made from the humerus-radius-ulna joint to the carpals. After the cut is made I immediately place a small amount of dry preservative on the incision. This keeps fluids from getting on any feathers. With the dry preservative in place, begin working your fingers underneath the skin. Separate the skin on the trailing side of the wing until you can see the feather quills. Then turn your attention to the leading side and gently work your fingers to the leading edge of the wing. It may be helpful to reapply dry preservative on these muscle groups from time to time. This will allow you a better grip on the slippery tissues.

Using the scalpel, begin cutting the muscle tissue free from the trailing side of the wing. Carefully cut until this tissue is loose. Then cut each end and any remaining points that you haven't already severed. After completing the trailing side turn your attention to the leading side. I like to start cutting this tissue free at the bone and then work my way forward. Cut straight down to the radius bone, then begin cutting the tissue free as you work toward the leading edge. You may have to use your fingers to help work the tissue free here. As it becomes loose, sever each end and pull it free. Continue by removing the section of tissue between the radius and ulna. This section may be the toughest to remove. I begin by making a cut on each side of the muscle section along each bone. Then I turn the scalpel at a slight angle and begin almost a prying action until I can get hold of this muscle with my hands. After I establish a good grip, I gently cut with the scalpel until it is free.

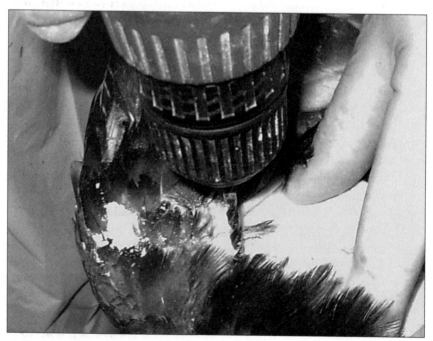

Drilling wingbone.

Continue preparing the wing area by removing the oils from inside the wing bones. To do this, simply drill a small hole on each end of both the radius and the ulna using a ⅛ or 3/16 drill bit. Be very careful not to drill through the outside of the wings. This may cause the oil within the bones to seep to the outside, which will in turn contaminate the feathers. You could also do damage to these small feathers. After the holes are drilled, cover one hole with a small cloth. Then place an air nozzle on the uncovered hole. Now gently blow the compressed air into the open hole. You may have to use your fingers to close off any air escaping around the nozzle. This will force the oil and marrow out of the bone. If left inside, these oils could eventually leak onto the feathers, causing what is termed in the taxidermy business as "grease burn." After proper cleaning, generously sprinkle this area with dry preservative.

Only one more part of the wing remains to be dealt with before we continue—the hand section, which is the last muscle-containing section in the wing. The hand is near the smallest section of the wing, near the end. This section is actually the "carpometacarpus." Use the scalpel to cut a small V between the two bones that make up this section. Lightly pry as you make several cuts on each side until the very small amount of tissue is free. Then pack the area with preservative. Complete both sides and continue.

Now you should be ready to wire the wings and legs. I usually start with the legs. Generally, when I use a leg-to-leg incision, I detach the legs completely from the skin. With the breast incision, I leave the legs attached. Before wiring the legs, the tendons on the back side must be removed. Start by making a small cut across the ball of the foot. Using a regulator, reach inside the incision and find the tendons. Slide the regulator under one or two of these tendons and pull them free. Don't attempt to pull too many tendons at one time; this may cause them to break. I have found it best to slide the regulator all the way through to the other side, place the ball of the foot between the ring and middle fingers, and pull. It may take some force to pull the first couple tendons free, but the rest will be easier to work on after these are removed. There should be a total of seven. After you pull the tendons free, cut them at the point where they continue into the foot.

Removing these tendons provides space for the leg wire to be inserted. The wire size you choose will vary depending on the

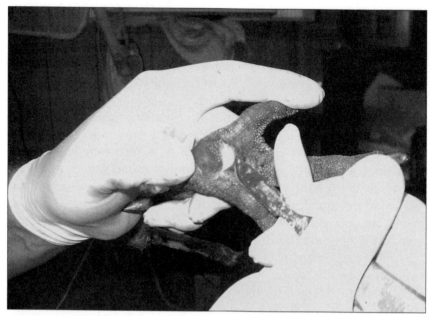

Cutting foot pad.

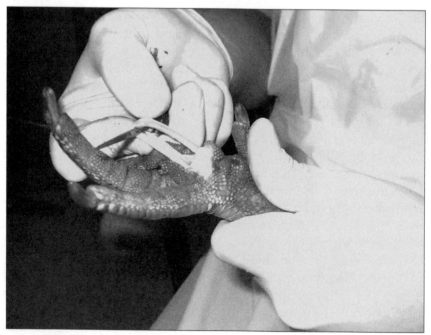

Removing tendons.

Cutting tendons.

pose. For a flying mount, the leg wire will only have to hold the legs up, as they won't support the weight of the mount. Therefore, when mounting a flying bird, I use size 10 wire for the legs. For a strutting, gobbling, or standing bird it is best to use size 8 wire because the leg wire will be used to hold the bird erect. When choosing a leg wire for a standing bird, keep in mind that it is best to use a size too large rather than too small.

To insert the wire it helps to sharpen one end. If the leg is attached to the skin, make sure the feathered skin is folded down around the scaled leg. Holding the leg in one hand and the wire in the other, insert the wire into the small cut made to remove the tendons. With all of the tendons removed, the wire should easily slide the distance of the scaled leg. If the wire is tough to insert you may not have removed all of the tendons. If you believe that they have all been removed and you are still having trouble, insert the blunt end of the wire into a cordless drill and cautiously push the wire into the leg while operating the drill. Be careful. If feathers get wrapped around the wire they may be pulled free or damaged.

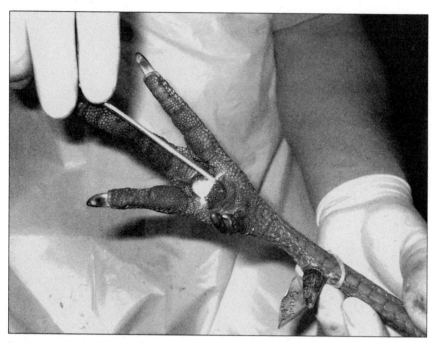

Inserting wire into leg.

It is much easier to insert this wire when using the leg-to-leg incision because no skin or feathers will get in the way. This allows you to concentrate on inserting the wire.

When the wire is completely inserted you are ready to restore the musculature of the leg. Before you continue to replace these muscles, make sure that enough wire is extending past the foot to properly secure the bird to a base. (If you have chosen a flying pose, the wire doesn't need to extend past the ball of the foot.) You should also ensure that enough wire extends past the leg bone or femur to positively anchor the leg.

Begin the rebuilding process by using some type of twine. I like to use a dark-colored yarn. It is inexpensive and plenty strong enough to accomplish the task. I use the dark color in case there are unnoticed holes in the legs or wings. White polyfil will be used, but at times you will use only the yarn, which will help with see-through holes.

To obtain the most accurate shape possible when rebuilding the muscle tissue you should—prior to removing the tissue—lay the leg

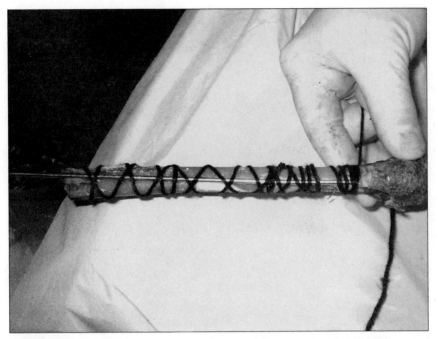

Wrap the leg bone to wire using twine. In this photo we have chosen yarn.

onto a sheet of paper or cardboard and trace its outline. Trace the leg while it is positioned on its side and then its back. This will give you a frontal shape as well as a side shape. Using your outlines as reference, begin forming the leg muscle.

After squeezing the leg bone and the wire together, begin wrapping from the scaled leg toward the end of the femur. I usually make several passes back and forth across the femur to ensure a good coupling. Now begin wrapping the femur and wire with polyfil. It is usually best to rebuild muscles slightly smaller rather than larger. This is to make sure that the skin will fit without a struggle. Forcing the skin around any muscle that is too large will likely cause problems later, primarily separation at the seams.

If you have chosen to leave the legs attached to the skin you will have to wait until the final mounting process begins before attaching them to the manikin. But if you are working with legs separate from the skin, now is a great time to attach them. Most quality bird manikins, whether they are waterfowl or upland birds, have designated spots for wire placement. These spots are usually small

Tracing both front and side views.

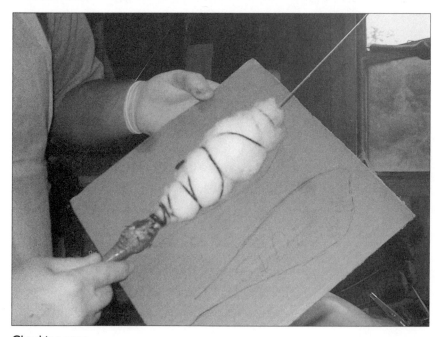

Checking wrap.

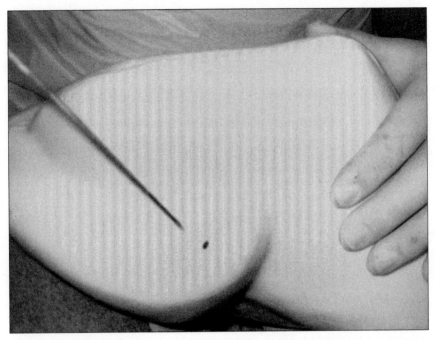

Inserting leg wire.

dimples in the wing pockets and the thigh area. Just find these dimples and force the sharpened end of the wire into each one. If the wire is tough to push through, use a small hammer to tap the wire's end or grip the wire with pliers and twist while pushing. If you are performing this operation with the manikin on your lap, be careful to keep your hands and legs out of the way.

Once the wire is completely through the manikin, twist the sharpened end into a U-shape. Tap this U back into the manikin, firmly anchoring the leg wire. Now slide the leg all the way to the pre-sculpted thigh. With the femur firmly seated against the thigh of the manikin, bend the leg to a correct anatomical position. Repeat this procedure on the opposite side and then attach the manikin with the legs to a base or drying board. It is sometimes easier to obtain a more accurate bird posture by using this method. Once the correct posture is obtained, you simply slide the skin on and continue the mounting process. You shouldn't have to move the position of the legs or the angle of the body to the legs very much to achieve a perfect balance.

Now turn your attention back to the wings. The wings can be wired in many different ways. I have found that a wire running the entire length of the wing bones will provide more control over the final product. This wire provides stability and easier positioning for the otherwise limp wing. You will need to determine the wire size at this time. Closed-wing turkeys won't need wire as large as that used for a flying pose. Generally speaking, I use size 8 or 10 gauge for flying and 10 or 12 for a closed-wing pose. The exact wire size usually depends on the size of the bird.

To insert the wire, slide it through the inside of the skin along the humerus, past the radius and ulna, and into the hand section. It's okay if the wire protrudes, as long as it can be cut after drying and easily hidden. Again, be very careful when inserting this wire. Holding the wing in one hand and the wire in the other, carefully work the wire in by twisting and pushing until the hand section, or carpometacarpus, is fully penetrated.

After you have attached the wire to the full length of the wing bones, secure it in place. Begin by wrapping the wire and the hu-

Before attaching to the wire, trim the excess edge of the ball on the humerus. This should help with a tight fit.

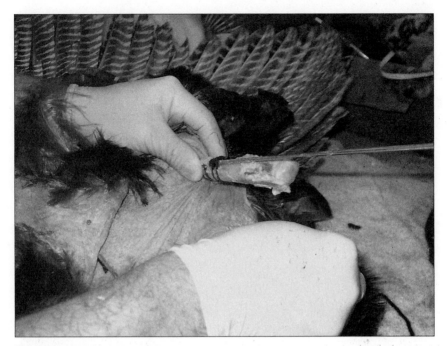

Wrapping wing bone using yarn.

merus several times at the humerus-radius-ulna joint. Wrap tightly, and then bring the wire around to the top side of the humerus. Continue wrapping the full length of the humerus. This wrap should be tight to prevent the wire from sliding around to the side of the humerus. Once the wrap is complete, begin adding a small amount of polyfil to the humerus to replace the wing muscle. Go light here, as too much will cause the finished mount to look bulky and unnatural. Again, by tracing the outline onto paper you will get a much truer shape when it is time to replace this tissue.

With the wing properly wired and wrapped, sew up the openings on the underside. In a closed-wing bird this isn't as important as in a flying pose, where the underside of each wing is easily visible. Now lay the wing out of the way and continue with the opposite side. With both sides complete, the skin is ready for mounting.

In recent years several top taxidermists have come up with their own turkey wing systems. One system involves completely skinning the wing to the wrist and removing the entire skeletal and muscular structure, and then replacing this structure with an artificial wing,

Sewing wing.

Incisions should be easily hidden.

which is flexible. This is a great method to use, but it may be best for first-timers to learn the method that uses the existing framework. It's good to know there are other options available, though, and as you progress you may want to choose a different procedure for handling the wings.

Next, the tail must be prepared for attachment. Refer to chapter 7, Fan and Cape Preparation, to prepare the tail with the bondo method. The only addition to the tail preparation here is that you will attach two lengths of wire that help hold the tail in place. These wires are sharpened and inserted about an inch from each side of the fan, just below the tail quills. With the tail spread, as for a strutting or flying pose, the wires will cross inside the manikin. This creates a great anchor point for the tail. After inserting the wires, and before the bondo is applied, use car wax to coat the ends of the wires that will be bedded into the bondo. This will allow you to slide the wires in and out, so you can tap them into place once the bondo has hardened.

Bondo fan for flying bird. Note the inserted wire, which will be used to anchor the tail in its finished position.

Another difference from the earlier discussion on tail preparation is that the tail will not be fixed flat. Instead, it will have a slight arch. This more closely simulates the position of the tail on a live bird, which you will quickly notice when studying live reference. To achieve this slight arch, (after applying the bondo) lay the tail quills on any object that will slightly lift the center. You may have to experiment with the thickness to obtain the proper arch. If the results do not meet your expectations simply remove the bondo before it hardens. Remember that removing bondo is simple in the first few stages of curing, but it becomes nearly impossible once it has been allowed to harden and cool.

When these steps are complete, you will be ready to continue with whatever pose has been selected.

10

Mounting a Flying Bird

One of my favorites poses—and the easiest life-sized mount to do accurately with the first attempt—is the flying bird. In a flying pose the turkey's body and wings are outstretched and his weight will not have to be distributed in any specific manner. This pose allows for more natural variables. After some solid reference study, this will become readily apparent.

In a mount where the turkey is displayed in a closed, standing position, there are many different points that must be accurately achieved. A good example of this is that when a bird stands, a certain amount of his body will be forward of his feet and a certain portion behind his feet. His body will also be held at a certain angle most of the time. This is for even weight distribution. Otherwise, the turkey would topple over. So poor balance in a mount will look unnatural. Also, when the wings are closed you must position them almost perfectly or you will have trouble positioning the adjoining feather tracts.

Besides being one of the easiest poses to pull off, a flying turkey is beautiful. Numerous customers bring their trophy to me each year, and for some reason the majority choose the strutting bird. It is understandable that the strutting bird is what every red-blooded turkey hunter wants to see when the bird is in its natural setting, but a flying mount shows the color of the spread feathers and the astoundingly large size of the outstretched bird.

Before reaching this point you should have already completed the pre-mounting procedures, which were detailed in the preceding chapter. You also should have the head painted (see chapter 12, Choosing and Painting a Head) and the proper manikin ready and all mounting supplies on hand.

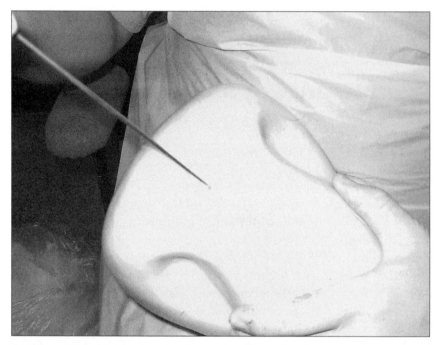

Attaching the neck wire is a simple matter of inserting the appropriate gauge of wire into the neck area. In the initial learning stages it may be easier to purchase a pre-manufactured neck for the chosen pose.

To begin the mounting process, insert the appropriate manikin, with the neck attached, into the skin. To prevent the neck wire from catching on the skin and making a hole, the end of the wire should be bent into the shape of a loop before insertion. Very carefully pull the neck skin onto the neck material, almost to the shoulders.

Find the small, pre-marked dimples that are located where the wing bone or humerus should attach. These marks are easily found in the forward part of the indentation between the breast and back. Once a spot is located, insert the wing wire and push until it protrudes from the opposite side. When the wire is visible use a pair of pliers to pull it until the humerus is flush with the manikin. Clip off the excess wire with a pair of cutting pliers. Use the pliers to bend the wire into an **L**, then bend the wire where it protrudes from the manikin, and lightly hammer the **L** into the manikin. This should lock the wing into place. After you are finished, make sure that the humerus is still flush with the manikin. Complete the opposite wing in the same manner.

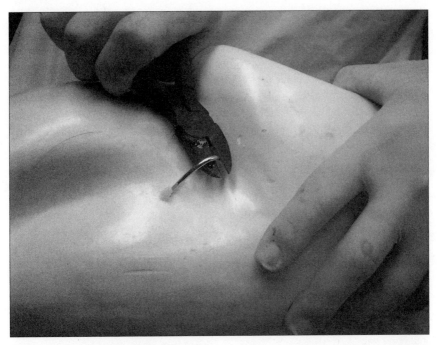

Then anchor into place (pre-mount).

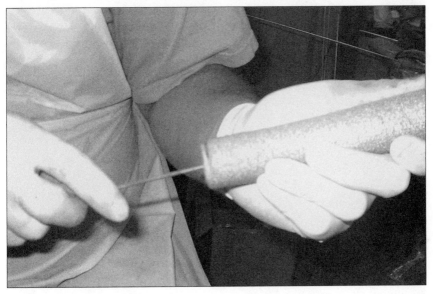

Finish by sliding on 8"–12" of 1⅛ neck material. You will later size the length to fit.

Inserting neck.

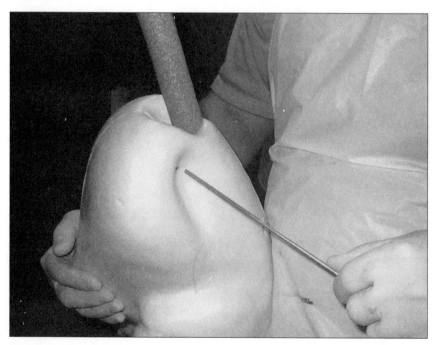

Inserting wing wire.

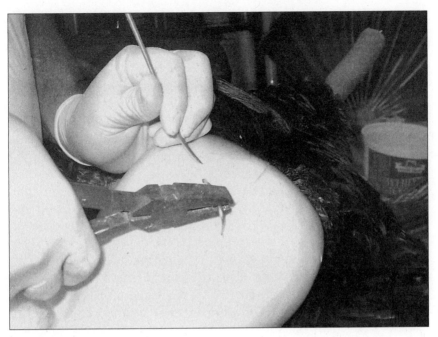

Anchoring wing wire.

Once the wings are attached securely, pull the skin onto the body a bit more. If you used the leg-to-leg incision and have already attached the severed legs you will continue by sliding the skin the full length of the manikin. Otherwise, if the legs are still attached to the skin, pull the skin the full length then pin the back skin up on the back several inches. This will allow the leg wires to exit the back of the manikin without damaging the skin.

Find the small dimples that are used to indicate proper placement of the wire. Now insert a leg wire into a dimple at an angle that will make the wire exit through the lower back. Form a U in the end of the wire and solidly hammer this into the manikin. With the base of the wire attached, slide the leg upward until it firmly contacts the manikin. Attach the other leg in a similar manner. Attaching the second leg may cause the skin to become tight, so proceed cautiously to avoid tearing anything. After both legs are attached, fully encase the manikin with the turkey skin. When this step is complete, you should have both legs and both wings attached and the skin should be ready to sew.

If you are using the breast incision and have chosen the correct manikin size, sewing should be easy. Find the X that was cut into the point of the breast. If you have unknowingly ripped past the X you will need to sew up the tear until you reach it. To continue, use pins to attach the pre-marked area to the point of the breast. Next, sew the skin slowly from the breast point toward the anal opening. While sewing, make certain each side is being joined evenly. Securely tie the thread off when you are finished. To tie off a seam simply insert the needle and pull it through without tightening the thread. Now insert your finger into the loose loop made by the last pass of the needle. Doing this will allow you to pull the seam tight. Remove the needle from the tag end and hold the loose thread end in the opposite hand. Finish by completing a simple overhand knot. Pull tight then repeat for a secure knot.

If you used the leg-to-leg incision there are a few minor differences in the sewing process. First, you must prepare the legs where the feathered skin joins the scaled leg. To make the joint look convincing you will need to build up the area next to the knee with epoxy, which can be purchased at most any taxidermy supply. I prefer the color black for this. I use Apoxie Sculpt, which is available in many colors. After mixing the colored epoxy, wrap a small portion just above the knee. Continue by pulling the skin around the leg and epoxy and then start sewing. Sew until you reach the middle of the breast. Start again on the opposite side with the same

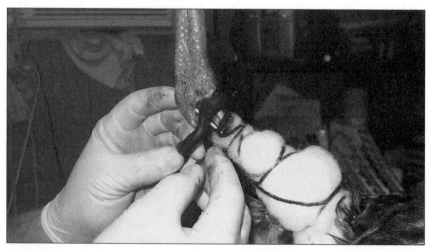

Wrap the joint area with a black epoxy. This should easily blend with the feathers should a small portion of underlying material show through.

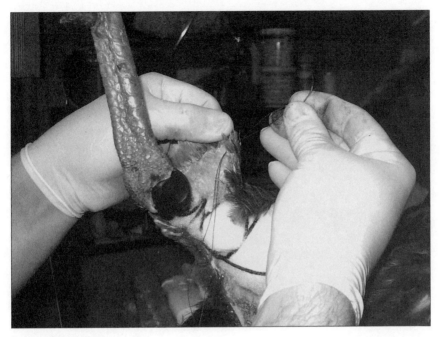

Sewing leg incision.

procedure. When you reach the center of the breast and the other sewed area, tie off the seam. Now the bird is ready to have the tail attached and posed.

Before going any further you will need to attach the turkey to a wire, which will secure your prize to a panel or piece of driftwood. Size 6 or 8 wire works best for this job. You need something sturdy to prevent problems when you attempt final positioning. Sharpen each end of the large wire and bend it into a square-bottomed U at its halfway point. After determining which direction you want the bird to face, insert the wire under the opposite wing. To insert the wire, move the wing out of the way toward the back. Then pull the breast feathers located under the wing forward slightly. This will expose bare skin. Begin pushing the two ends of wire into this area, angling toward the peak of the breast area in the middle of the body. Using a hammer, lightly tap the end of the wire until the sharpened ends are showing on the opposite side of the breast. By tapping, pushing, and pulling, insert the wire the entire distance until the bottom of the square-shaped U is flush to the body. Bend the wires where they exit the body and attach the turkey to either a panel or a small piece of plywood. First, pre-drill two holes a size

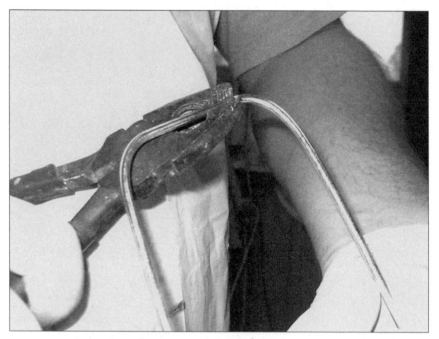

Bending the flying bird body wire into shape.

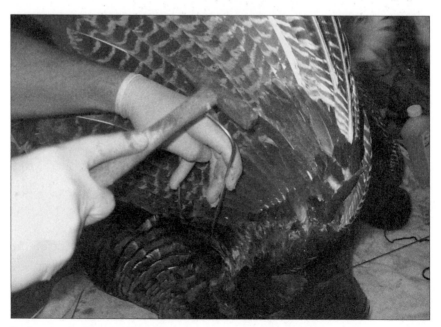

Body wire for hanging flying mount.

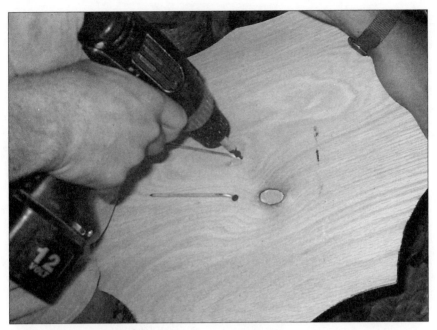

After inserting and bending wire, insert screws to anchor the wire.

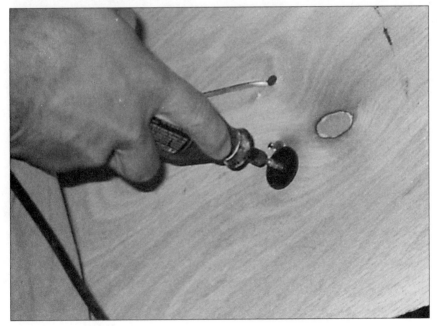

After anchoring with screws, use a Dremel cutoff tool to cut excess wire.

larger than the wire used to attach the turkey. The wires shouldn't have a lot of play, but they should slide easily into place. After the wires are inserted, bend them at right angles, which helps hold the bird in position. By attaching the flying bird to a panel now, you can avoid the step of moving the bird from a piece of scrap wood to a panel later on.

The easiest approach is to attach the turkey and panel or plywood to a mounting stand. If you do not have one you will have to work on a bench. This isn't impossible, but a stand is helpful. If you use a stand be careful not to screw the attachment screws through the front of the panel.

To attach the tail, push the turkey skin surrounding the tail junction up out of the way. Using a small dull knife, widen and deepen the V that already exists in the tail area of the manikin. Try to keep this V the same angle as the preexisting one. Your objective is to allow extra room for the bondo and wires that have been added to support the tail. Use the mounted tail to periodically check for a proper fit. When the tail slides easily into the V, find the correct

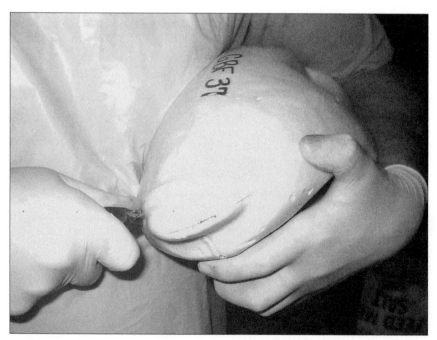

Sometimes cutting the tail slot prior to mounting is best.

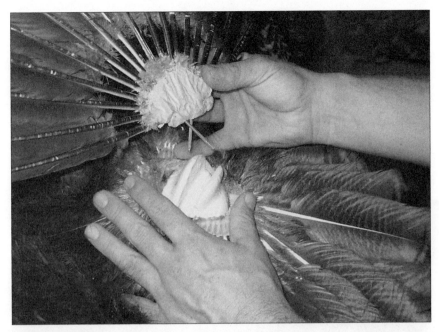

Tail attachment.

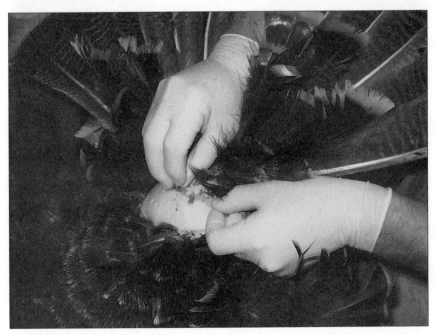

Pinning tail skin.

This should be an easily hidden seam.

angle for the tail and tap the two wires within the tail section into the manikin. This will properly anchor the tail in place.

Finish the tail junction by pinning the skin of the tail and the skin of the body together. This junction is easily hidden, but try to join the two skins evenly and securely. Start with the tail section, first the top then the bottom. Finish by attaching the body skin in the same sequence. Try to match up the areas that were originally cut apart.

Complete the turkey by attaching the head. (Refer to chapter 12, Choosing and Painting a Head, for instructions on preparing the head.)

PRESERVING THE FEET

Before continuing the final posing process it is necessary to preserve the feet. Numerous liquid preservatives are available. An inexpensive but effective and readily available chemical for preservation is denatured, or wood, alcohol. Denatured alcohol is available at most hardware stores. To use this or any other preservative, you will have to inject it into several areas of the feet. Caution should be used here. Wear proper hand and eye protection. Also, don't use any type of chemical in an enclosed area.

If you choose a preservative from a taxidermy supplier follow the directions for its use; most are used full strength. You can use denatured alcohol at full strength, or you can cut it 50 percent with water. Many taxidermists use denatured alcohol and cut the strength by half. This is generally believed to be potent enough for preservation. Also, because their workload is high, cutting the alcohol increases its volume, which saves money.

A syringe will be necessary to inject the liquid. A small syringe is fine and these can be obtained from a taxidermy supply company or at a farm or veterinary supply house.

Fill the syringe with preservative and inject the feet. Be very careful when handling any needle and while injecting. Sometimes

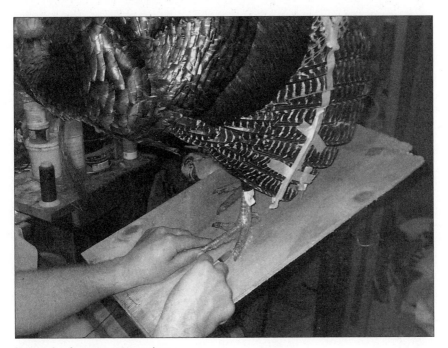

Inject the feet in various places.

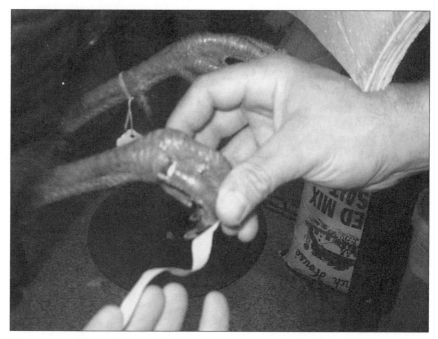

After preserving a flying bird's feet, they should be taped closed. This is how a bird holds its feet while in flight.

the injected fluid will have nowhere to go, forcing pressure to build that may spray you in the face. Always wear eye protection.

Start injecting between each toe. Continue on the side of each toe, almost halfway to the toenail. Inject about one cc into each toe. Now move up the leg and inject one to two cc's at the base of the rear toe. Moving up the leg, inject two to three areas until the entire scaled leg has been completed. Just insert the needle under the scale in the chosen area and inject as usual.

If the syringe becomes difficult to use during the injection process, the chosen area could be full or a hard area encountered. If you feel the area has obtained at least a portion of the recommended dosage, move on. If you weren't able to inject any preservative, try to find a more receptive location in the immediate area.

With the head and tail attached and the feet preserved, it is time to finish the mount by positioning and grooming. Because the feathers and wings will tend to give in to gravity we will use wire, tape, and string to hold them in position while they dry.

To begin final positioning make sure the legs are pulled up to the breast and almost together. Again, refer to reference material to achieve the correct angles and positioning. Usually, the toes will be closed when a turkey flies. Sometimes masking tape is needed to help the toes maintain a closed position.

Now place the wings at the desired angle. This angle may vary quite a bit depending on how aggressively the turkey is flying. In a gliding position, the wings will be more relaxed and to the side, but a turkey just taking flight will be more aggressive, with wings farther forward and outstretched. Either way is correct. A good starting point is to extend the wings to the side. Both wings need to look even, holding in the same plane.

A good reference for the location of the wings is to make sure the secondary feathers, the ones closest to the body, are touching the sides of the body and slightly overlapping the tail feathers. As stated earlier, the wings can vary a great deal, but this is a good place to start. As you gain experience you may want to study various flying positions and change the position and angle of the wings. After extending the wings to the desired location, add wire supports underneath them.

Using 12- or 14-gauge wire, make an insertion underneath the trailing end of the wing feathers. Then bend the wire to allow the trailing feathers to fall at the correct angle to the body. To insert this wire, sharpen one end then insert it into the manikin next to the back feathers, above the thigh area. Bend the wire sharply at first so the secondary wing feathers almost flow into the back feathers. Shape the remainder of the wire so it gradually slopes downward toward the wing tip. Attach the wire to the wing tip using masking tape. Now use the masking tape to evenly space the wing feathers. The wing feathers will overlap next to the body, but a gap will develop as you near the first primary. Using the wire and masking tape, position each wing to look proportionate and even to the opposite side.

If you used the bondo method to prepare the tail, each feather should overlap or lie underneath the next, depending on which direction the tail is flowing. However, if a tail feather is unruly use the masking tape to lock it into position.

Now go to the shoulders of the turkey and begin positioning the shoulders, neck, and head. You will notice from looking at reference photos that each feather tract joins with no spaces or feather

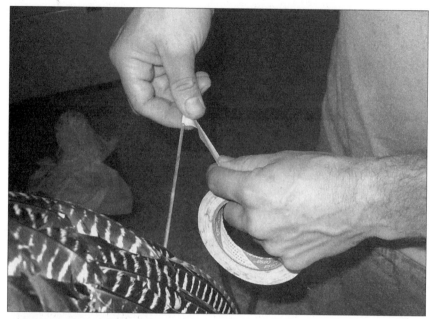

Attaching tape to wire's end will provide an additional anchor point for the tape, which will hold the wing primaries in position.

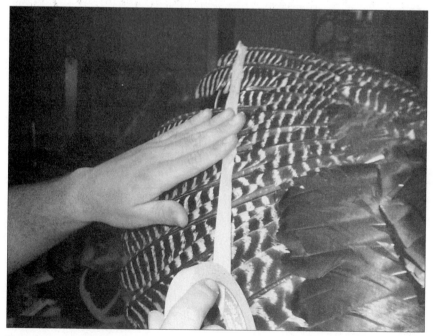

Taping wing feathers.

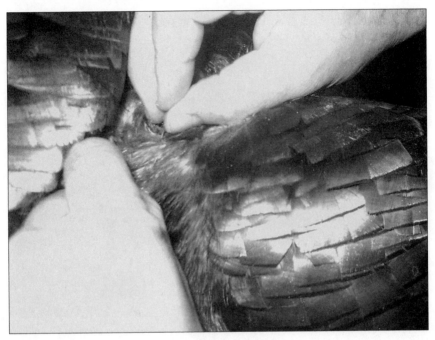

Pin together feather tracts until no down is visible.

down showing between tracts. Using reference, you will notice a small line that extends down the center of the breast. You will also notice lines on either side of the head going toward the wings. If you create these lines in a gently flowing manner the mount will be much more convincing. To ensure this kind of junction it will probably be necessary to pin each tract together.

Start by finding the scapulars, which are atop the shoulder areas. When the wings were extended the scapulars may have been pulled away from the body. To correct this, pull the scapulars back to the turkey manikin and pin them. After pinning, the back feathers should flow into the scapulars with no separations. Also, the breast feathers may have fallen away. Repeat the previous procedure by pulling the area underneath and forward of the shoulder upward to the shoulder area. Then pin it to lock this feather tract into position. Continue by grooming the feathers toward the head. If there is a small gap between feather tracts, groom the feathers of each tract toward one another.

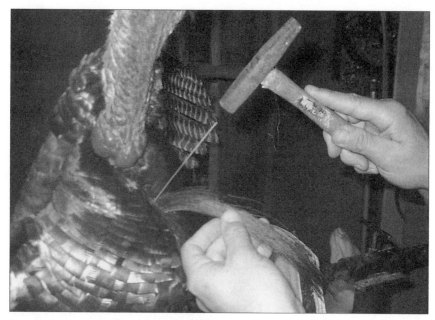

It is sometimes best to anchor the beard on either a flying or strutting bird. This will ensure proper angle and alignment.

A completed mount.

Now turn your attention to head and neck posture. A good position to start with for a flying bird is to angle the body slightly upward with the head and neck area almost level with the floor. To achieve this look, bend the head down and gently away from the wall. Also, the head will need to be swiveled gently in the opposite direction from which the turkey is posed.

With the feathers groomed and the body positioned, place the turkey out of the way. Allow it to sit for at least two weeks. Check the posture and feather placement every day, especially during those critical first few days.

11

Mounting a Strutting Bird

The initial mounting procedures for a strutting bird are almost the same as those for a flying bird. The exception is a small layer of polyfil that you will slide between the manikin and the turkey skin to help hold the back feathers erect as the bird dries. Without this material, the feathers tend to lie down.

The first few steps for preparing the strutting bird mount are briefly described below. For a more thorough account of these initial procedures, refer to chapter 10, Mounting a Flying Bird.

Begin by laying the prepped and wired bird on its back. Attach the wing wires and then slide in a strutting manikin of the correct size with an artificial neck attached.

Before attaching the leg wires, insert a thin layer of polyfil along the center of the back. Do this by tearing off a sheet of polyfil about 4 to 5 inches wide and 18 inches long. Thin the polyfil by cutting the thickness in half. Insert the material underneath the back skin. Make sure the polyfil extends all the way to the neck area of the manikin and pin it in place. Pull the skin over the material and continue positioning it. Now attach the leg wires to finish the last of the wire connections. Sew the incision and continue with the posing process.

Position the bird by placing it on a base or a piece of plywood. When posing the turkey I don't like to place the feet side by side. In my opinion, this gives the mount a stale look. Placing one foot forward, as if the bird were walking, helps bring it to life. To get an accurate placement of the feet, experiment until a look matches your reference. Roughly position the feet with the leg wires extending in a straight line from the bottom of the feet, mark the spot on the chosen base material, and then drill holes of the proper size.

If you choose to place the turkey directly on the final base at this stage, it is best to roughly position the feet on a piece of scrap plywood first. This will prevent your having to fill the final base with a number of holes while you determine an appropriate position for the feet. Once you have the position you want, transfer the location of the leg wire holes to the permanent base.

Whether you choose a temporary or permanent base, a secure attachment will have to be made. Flush the feet to the base, bend the wires out of the way, and screw 1½-inch screws into the same hole the wire exits. This locks the wire into place. If the base is temporary, leave the excess wire attached. If the base is permanent, cut the excess wire. (This process is covered in detail in chapter 13, Base Building 101.)

Following proper feet placement, the legs should be adjusted so as not to look rigid. Do this by bending the leg at the thigh and upper leg joint, then again where the feathers meet the scales. Make small adjustments. Don't bend the legs too much, as this will give the bird a crouched look. On the other hand, a straight leg also looks abnormal.

Next, start roughly positioning the body posture using the photo reference of a live strutting turkey. Using a side profile photo, place a straightedge horizontally through the body. This will allow you to capture the approximate angle of the body while the turkey is in a strut position. You should be able to get the body very close to the correct angle, but you will probably end up slightly shifting the body by the end of the posing process.

Now attach the tail. To prep the tail slot for insertion of the fan, use a dull paring knife to widen the pre-positioned **V**. Widen and deepen the tail slot so that it easily accommodates the fan base. Be careful not to alter the angle of this slot. Turkeys can shift their tail from side to side and slightly forward and back on each side, but these advanced poses are best left until you have gained more experience. For beginners, it will be best to follow the guidelines of the pre-sculpted slot. When the fan slides easily into place anchor it with the two crossing wires that were already inserted into the base of the tail.

With the tail anchored securely, pin the skin of the tail to the manikin. Continue pinning the loose skin as you move to the underside of the tail. Now center the back feathers of the body skin and pin them into place. Finish by pinning the body skin underneath the tail. Make certain the skin is pinned thoroughly and that no gaps exist between the tail and body skin.

After thoroughly attaching each skin area, grasp the small feathers that appear underneath the tail and pull them downward. These feathers hang down when a bird is strutting, although most people won't notice this minor detail of the mount. Still, all the reference I have used depicts these small feathers in a downward position.

Now turn your attention to the wings. Obviously, a turkey will drop his wing tips as he struts, dragging them along the ground. This is a very controlled position and the wings aren't merely dropped to the ground. Most of the action is achieved with the primaries. The secondary feathers maintain a closed position similar to that of a standing bird. To re-create this, follow your reference closely. Begin by placing the humerus into the pocket that is sculpted in the manikin. When you have attached one end of the humerus with wire, the loose end will need to be bent into place along this same plane. Bend the wing and make sure the humerus-radius-ulna joint is positioned very close to the body. Then get a rough position by

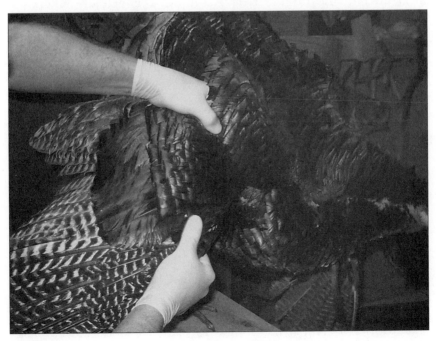

Shaping wing.

pulling the hand section of the wing downward. Do this gradually, until the leading primary feather touches the base. This should create a position very close to what you'll want. Repeat this procedure with the opposite wing, and then move on to the head.

The head will be pulled down and into the forward area of the back. Be careful not to add too much neck while attaching the head. When adjusting the length of the neck, I believe it is better to be an inch short than an inch long. According to reference, most strutting turkey heads never reach above the raised back feathers. Several adjustments may need to be made before the exact position is determined.

Now use a regulator to pull the back feathers forward. This will begin to layer the feathers, and although they will not continue to stand, they will begin to lose their flat appearance. Proceeding to the front of the bird, fluff the feathers in the same manner. It might help to use a hair dryer to further dry and fluff the feathers at this point. The feathers seem to be easier to dry with the skin on a manikin than when lying flat and bunched together.

At this time, I begin to pin any excess skin that remains in the front area of the turkey. Before any slack is actually taken up, though, I pin the area that belongs on the point of the breast to the point of the manikin. This will reduce any shift that might result from pulling the feather tracts from one side to the other. There may be sagging in the breast area, especially if a slightly smaller form was chosen. This is fine, as it can be reduced by pinning up the area under each wing. Don't lift the wing too much while pinning the skin in place. This might alter the rough positioning work you've already completed. Reach under each wing and feel for the portion of the featherless skin near the attachment point between the wing and the body. Stick a pin into the skin and lift it until the breast area shows very little sag. Continue placing several pins on each side in the same manner until the skin is secure.

Now finish positioning the wings. Sharpen one end of a 24-inch piece of 12- or 14-gauge wire. Insert the sharpened end into the manikin near the edge of the back feathers, just forward of the tail. After inserting the wire a couple of inches, bend it down toward the base. Very carefully pull the secondary and primary feathers around to the top of the wire, and wedge the wire onto the base to form a small outward arch. If the arch is too large, continue to cut short

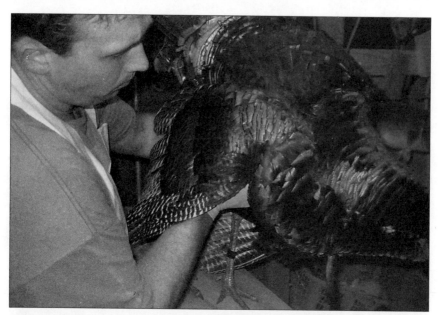

Pinning the skin underneath the wing—alongside the breast.

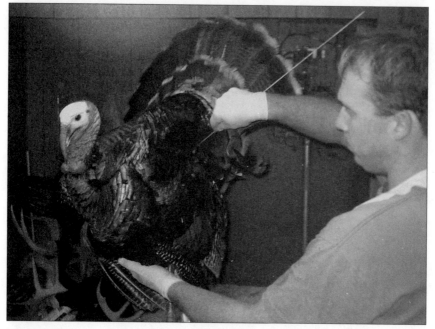

Insertion of wire adjacent to the back feathers will allow a solid anchor for the tape that will be used to properly position the wing primaries.

lengths of wire until the wire forms a shape that resembles the natural arch in a turkey's wing as it is extended for strutting.

Finish posing the wing by applying masking tape to the wire as it enters the manikin. Then attach the tape to the secondary feathers. The secondary feathers should be much closer together than the primaries during this final positioning. Using reference, you will notice that most secondary feathers are near the back, tucked almost up to the spread tail, while the primary feathers begin to spread gradually as they near the base or ground. Position the wing feathers similar to reference, then lock them into place using the masking tape you just applied to the attachment point of the wire. Gradually work your way down the wing feathers, attaching the tape to each, then attach the tape to the underlying wire. Repeat this procedure for both wings, then stand back and make sure both sides are even. Look from the rear to check that both secondary groups match up and that both primary groups extend down the same amount. Also, make certain that one wing doesn't flair more than the other. Now look from the side and make any other necessary adjustments.

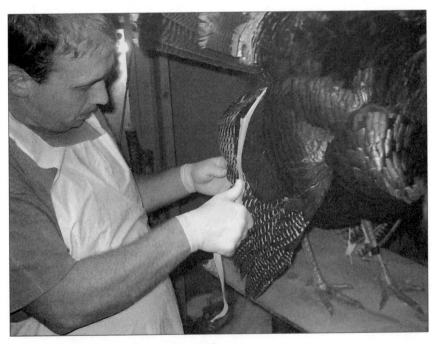

Position each primary, then anchor with tape.

Next, the scapulars, or shoulder feathers, need to be pinned into position. Stick the edge of the scapular feathers with a pin and pull them over the wing manikin junction. Pin into place, then lightly groom the area. If the positioning is right, the feathers of the back will flow into the scapulars. To ensure proper positioning, make certain that no feather down is visible. Now pull the breast area feathers, located below and forward of the wing connection, up to the starting point of the scapular feathers. Pin the skin in this location. Repeat the same procedures for the opposite wing and continue grooming the feathers along the area joining the two feather tracts.

When using reference you will notice that these adjoining areas appear as lines. One line goes down the center of the breast and others extend from each side of the head. Studying reference will show you that these lines are symmetrical on each side. To create a good, natural look, make certain these same lines are closely reproduced in the mount. Once you have the lines even, gently groom the feathers together. Be certain to eliminate any gaps or feather down that may show.

Pinning scapulars.

The mount is almost complete. All that remains is the minor adjustments that may be needed according to your reference. Also, the mount will need the puffed look associated with a strutting turkey. Many taxidermists achieve this look by attaching the mount to the ceiling upside down as it dries. This raises the back feathers necessary for a strutting mount, but it does very little to fluff the breast feathers. I tried correcting this by attaching a strutting turkey to the wall in the drying stage, but this seemed to shove the feathers too far forward. I eventually settled on positioning my strutting birds at a 45-degree or slightly larger angle. This seems to pull the feathers nicely forward without overdoing it.

If you have an adjustable mounting stand, attach the base to the stand then adjust the stand to the proper angle. If you don't have a stand, you can firmly attach a 2 × 4 between the wall and the floor at the desired angle and then attach the turkey. If you use the latter method, be sure that the 2 × 4 is firmly fixed to both the wall and the floor to avoid any mishap that could damage the turkey. Place the turkey in an out of the way area, because you'll be leaving it in this position for at least two weeks.

With the turkey in its final position, begin pulling the back feathers forward with a regulator. These back feathers will quickly begin to stand on their own. Now use the regulator to pull the breast feathers forward, letting them fall back into position. This will give the breast area a slight shingling effect. Continue to check the turkey daily for any problem areas.

When all positioning is finished, the feet should be preserved. You can do this at any stage, but now is an ideal time. This procedure is detailed in chapter 10, Mounting a Flying Bird.

The turkey should dry thoroughly within two to three weeks, at which point you can continue with finishing and proper base attachment, if you haven't already done so.

12

Choosing and
Painting a Head

Up to this point, our focus has centered on the turkey skin because without clean, intact plumage a mount's quality suffers tremendously. However, another integral part of a mount is the brightly colored head for which these spring monarchs are so renowned. With the wild turkey's patriotic red, white, and blue head, it is easy to see why Benjamin Franklin wanted to make this our national bird.

Because of these bright colors, the head is obviously one of the first things an onlooker will notice about your trophy. It also brings this ball of feathers to life. Whether the head is painted and attached properly can mean the difference between a great mount— one that you proudly display—and one that is better off hidden in the closet.

In the previous chapters, we simply detached the head and put it aside to deal with later, but proper care at these initial stages is very important to the finished product. There are several options in dealing with the head, and it's time to take a look at the pros and cons for each method.

1. Have a reputable freeze-dry service mount and preserve your turkey head.

This is my favorite method for a lifelike look. I have several turkey mounts in my shop, some with freeze-dried heads and some with artificial heads. The turkey head question always seems to arise when a customer comes in to look around. They may not even be considering a turkey mount, but they notice the different heads and ask about them. After I offer a brief explanation of what the difference is, most choose their favorite. I can't recall anyone who has preferred the artificial over the freeze-dried head.

The prices of freeze-drying services vary, but they are usually comparable to artificial heads or slightly higher. The average price is currently around $35.

One disadvantage of using a freeze-drying service is product turnaround. Because they service taxidermists nationwide, you must wait your turn. These turnaround times vary with the season and workload, but you can expect eight weeks at best. And if you want freeze drying completed in the peak of the turkey-mounting season it may be four to six months. To find out exactly how long it will be, call the service ahead of time. Most are honest and will try to be exact with projected turnaround; their reputation is riding on it. Also, if you explain to them that you have only one or two heads they may work you in. Should you need a freeze-dried head immediately, most freeze driers have spares. Obviously, these heads will not be from your turkey, but neither will an artificial.

Another disadvantage is that if you damage your turkey head severely with the shot it may be rendered useless. In this case, your only alternative is a surplus freeze-dried head or an artificial one. There are very few heads that don't require at least minor repairs from holes created by pellets. Depending on the severity of the damage, a repair might be minimal or it could be painstaking and still net less than perfect results.

If you decide to have your turkey head freeze dried, it should be properly prepared for shipment. Begin by placing the head in a plastic bag. Zip-Loc bags are useful for this. Usually, a head will fit into a pint-sized or sandwich-sized bag. The only drawback to the sandwich bag is that the walls are much thinner, leaving them vulnerable to punctures. If you can find the pint-sized freezer bags, they are probably a better choice. With the head already inside, fill the bag with water. Don't overfill, as this will only cost more to ship, but make sure the head is completely covered with water. This is also a great way to store a head. I have kept heads that weren't going to be used for up to six months with no problems.

I like to insulate the box with crushed newspaper and send the heads for overnight or second-day delivery. Without expedited delivery, the heads may get ruined.

A good freeze-drying service to start with is Noonkester Freeze Drying Service. I recently started using their services and the quality has been great. They are also less expensive than some of their competitors. To contact them, call 1-800-888-3706.

2. Purchase a freeze drier and learn the freeze-drying method yourself.

Although I like to have my heads freeze dried, I prefer to send them off for several reasons. One reason is cost. Even the low-end freeze driers I have priced were upwards of $8,000. This is obviously a very large investment. Then you must learn how to properly operate it, which can be a lengthy process. I know of taxidermists who mount a hundred or more turkeys per year who still choose to send their heads out. They concentrate their efforts on the mounting techniques and let the freeze-drying experts do their job.

3. Purchase a commercially made artificial head.

While I feel the freeze-dried product is superior, there is no denying that the artificial heads of today are much better than those produced even 10 years ago. In my opinion, today's artificial heads look great. Don't confuse looking great with being comparable to a freeze-dried head, though. It just means that an artificial head that has been properly painted and attached can be quite convincing.

There are several methods for improving the look of an artificial head. One is to carefully blend the colors applied to it. This holds true for a freeze-dried version too; a head that looks painted looks fake—period. Another trick is to pull several hairs and small feathers from the original head using tweezers, and then use a small amount of Elmer's glue to attach them. Attach these feathers and hairs along the back of the neck and in the ears. This increases the head's natural look tenfold.

Artificial heads do have advantages. One huge advantage is that it will usually arrive within a week of ordering. Just pick a pose and order the head along with the manikin and other supplies. Also, no repairs need to be made on an artificial. They are ready to paint when they arrive. I have seen very few freeze-dried heads that didn't require at least slight repair.

4. Conventionally mount the head.

This is an option, but I wouldn't recommend it. I am sure that many bird taxidermists in the past used this method. Some may have enjoyed okay results; it's all what you get used to. My only attempt at a conventionally mounted head was horrific. The head looked good at first. Things changed quickly, though. The shrink-age was unbelievable. It would have taken a lengthy repair job to even get the head to resemble a turkey's. I quickly cut the head free and attached an artificial. The freeze-dried or artificial head is a much better choice than a conventionally mounted head.

After weighing these options, you must choose the type of head that best suits your needs and prepare it for attachment. Whether you choose an artificial or freeze-dried version it will have to be painted—unless you purchase one of the pre-painted heads. Pre-painted heads make things easy, but there is satisfaction in applying the convincing colors on your own.

Pre-painted heads do have their advantages. Because the people who color these heads do large quantities, they usually have a great natural color. Also, not having to worry about head painting will allow you to devote more time to learning taxidermy skills. Many taxidermists opt for a pre-painted head for their first turkey mount, letting head painting wait until their mounting skill improves.

For those who choose to tackle this project right away but might be afraid to start, know that head painting isn't rocket science. Be-cause the color of a turkey's head changes with its mood, no one color combination is always right or wrong. Also, the colors will dif-fer slightly from one bird to another. For the most part, head color is determined by the reference on hand and personal preference. Some taxidermists like a bright red head, some don't. Remember to trust your reference photos. If you happen to like a particular pic-ture, try to duplicate those colors.

EQUIPMENT NEEDS

Before you get started you need a thorough understanding of an airbrush. The cost range for airbrushes is from $40 to almost $300. While it is true that you get what you pay for, a beginner doesn't necessarily need everything a $300 airbrush has to offer. More ex-pensive models offer more adjustments to accommodate those with advanced skills. Also, the most expensive models are able to paint lines so thin you can barely see them for finesse detailing; a benefit that is definitely not necessary for a beginner.

For someone just learning bird or mammal taxidermy, I would recommend a single action Paasche airbrush. Single action means that once air is supplied and paint is attached all you have to do is press the trigger and paint. The flow is regulated with a twisting nozzle on the front of the brush. These airbrushes are the simplest to use, offer good results, and only cost around $40. Paasche has a firm reputation in the airbrushing industry, and their products will last a lifetime if cared for properly.

Now the proper colors must be chosen. As previously stated, there are no truly right or wrong colors. The basics are red, white, and blue, although the shades of each can vary drastically. I would suggest starting with the paints and colors I recommend. As you acquire more knowledge you can either modify this schedule or come up with one of your own.

Many years ago taxidermists simply used whatever paints were available. These days, taxidermists are able to purchase specially blended and formulated paints specifically for animal artistry. I have always used Lifetone paints for restoring color in my mounts. These

Materials needed for painting a freeze-dried head.

are lacquer based and will dry quickly after each application. For health concerns, many choose Hydromist, which are water-based paints. Other paints are available, but I am content with the quality I can achieve with these. To match the colors I recommend, you must either use the Lifetones or Hydromist or obtain a conversion chart for the paints that you choose.

The paints required to finish both the head and the feet include #503-sailfish blue, #504-pale blue, #101-gill red, #702-pure white. In addition to these colors you will need #100, which is a basecoat sealer, and a small amount of lacquer thinner. Start out by purchasing 8-ounce bottles. This amount will be enough for many heads.

PAINTING THE HEAD

Preparation for each head is slightly different. When prepping a freeze-dried head, use a small wire brush to thoroughly clean any

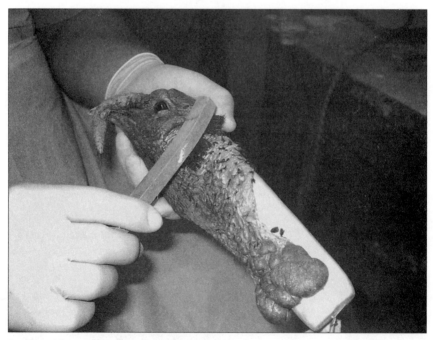

Brushing the head free of any loose skin.

loose skin that could flake off later and remove the overlying paint. Also, with a freeze-dried head, any shot holes will have to be filled with epoxy. Knead the two-part epoxy of your choice, plug the holes, and use a brush to blend the epoxy into the head. When you are finished the epoxy should have the same texture as the surrounding skin. Freeze-dried heads come with glass eyes already installed.

To prep an artificial head, all that should be needed is a good rubdown with a rag slightly dampened with lacquer thinner. Check for cracks that may appear in the head. If you happen to find a damaged area that requires more than a simple patching, return it to the supplier. Also, an artificial head usually comes without eyes. The eye you choose will dictate the proper time for insertion. I prefer glass eyes, as I consider them more realistic and lifelike. "Flex eyes" are also available, and they are easier to install. If you choose to use a flex eye, I would recommend painting the head before attaching the eyes. This will prevent your having to remove paint from the eye. Flex eyes, as the name implies, are flexible and slide easily into the sockets once the head has been painted.

If you choose glass you will need to grind away the eyelid, insert the eye, then attach a flex eyelid. (These are manufactured by the makers of flex eyes.) After you insert the glass eye with the new lid, the painting process can continue.

When using glass eyes in either the artificial or freeze-dried head you must avoid getting paint on the eye. Use a toothpick or small brush to apply an eye protection cream or Vaseline to the eye prior to the painting process. You also can remove the paint from the eye after the head has been painted.

After the prep work is finished, painting procedures are the same for either type of head. Remember to wear gloves while painting to avoid contact with the solvents. Also, it will make cleanup much easier.

To begin, thoroughly thin a small portion of sailfish blue. If you are using Lifetone, or any other lacquer-based paint, add lacquer thinner. If you have chosen Hydromist, or another water-based paint, add water or acetone. Paint the entire head with a medium coat of the thinned sailfish blue, being sure to avoid the beak. If you do get overspray on the beak remove it with a brush or Q-tip dipped in solvent. After the sailfish blue is dry, use a rag with solvent to wipe off the head. This is called a "blue wash." A blue wash

Spray sailfish blue over entire head. This will then be wiped off with either lacquer thinner or acetone depending on the type of paint used.

saturates the small wrinkles and crevices. When the other colors are applied the paints will have more of a blended effect.

After the sailfish blue has been removed, it is a good idea to seal the head with a basecoat sealer. This will give additional paints a good surface to which they can adhere. Apply two or three light coats.

Next, thoroughly paint the entire head, except for the crown and cheek, using the gill red paint. This red should be applied more heavily to the waddles and the front half of the head. The red will fade to a very light coat on the back half of the head. The snood should also be painted, and the color should extend lightly to the forward portion of the crown. This allows for proper blending, which should be your goal throughout the entire painting process.

Continue by mixing one part sailfish blue to four parts pale blue. This mixture can be varied some to match any reference or color preference you have. For darker blue, use more sailfish blue; for a lighter blue, use less. When you have the correct shade begin painting the rear half of the head and neck, blending into the red at the halfway mark. Avoid painting the crown, cheek, snood, or waddles, and apply this blue sparingly. Also, try to minimize the paint applied to the raised fleshy areas on the rear of the neck. In most reference you will notice that these raised areas are more red

Use gill red to paint the entire head except for the crown and cheek. This coat should be heavier on the front half of the head, fading to almost nothing on the rear of the head. Be sure to include the snood.

Apply one part sailfish blue mixed with 4 parts pale blue on the rear half of the head. Avoid painting the crown, cheek, snood, or waddles. Blend into the red at the halfway point.

than blue. To help with the application of this blue, adjust the nozzle to a narrow width and spray between each wrinkle. Don't worry if you happen to paint a high area blue. These colors vary and bleed naturally into each other on a live bird. In fact, it is best not to have harsh lines of definition.

Finish by painting the cheek and crown. Use sailfish blue to paint the cheek. Lightly spray the cheek, blending into the crown and neck area. Then add light layers until the cheek area looks natural. Now paint the crown using pure white, again blending to the surrounding colors. A good method of application is to paint at an angle. This will allow the underlying paint to show. Apply more heavily in the middle of the crown, lightening as you start into the snood area. A good blend can be achieved on the back of the neck by very lightly misting the white about a third of the way down. This white application on the back of the neck will be almost unnoticeable, but it helps blend the colors.

You can stop now or try to enhance your turkey head just a bit. I continue by using the gill red again to lightly touch up around the eyelid. Overspray onto the eye is fine, as it will either be protected or cleaned later. If you prefer a purple color on the cheek area, very lightly mist this red over the blue that has already been applied. This will darken the cheek.

One more color will help hide the transition from the head to the skin if the two happen to separate during the drying process. Using a black or dark brown color, spray the light colored head manikin that extends from the freeze-dried head. Be careful not to get paint on the skin, as this could be detrimental to a quality paint job. You may even choose to paint this area before the head-painting process begins.

I prefer to remove the paint from the eye after the head is finished. A turkey eye is very small and can be quickly dabbed with a Q-tip dipped in lacquer thinner—or acetone if you choose Hydromist. Don't get too close to the edge, as you might remove the paint from the eyelid. Remove the bulk of the paint from the center of the eye, and finish by using a scalpel to remove the rest along the edge of the eye.

Don't worry about painting the head perfectly on your first attempt. The paints can be removed easily using the proper solvent for your paint. After cleaning, you can simply start again. No problem.

Lightly paint the cheek surrounding the eye with sailfish blue.

Finish by using pure white to paint the crown, blending it into the surrounding colors. Tip: The raised nodules on the back of the head and neck should vary, some blue, some red. To achieve this, you may have to go back over some raised areas with an opposing color.

HEAD ATTACHMENT

The reason head attachment is included in the painting section rather than with the mounting instructions for each type of pose is that the procedure is the same. Sure, the positions are different, but the steps are identical. There are two different methods for attaching freeze-dried heads and artificial heads.

In my opinion, the artificial is much easier to attach. After obtaining a proper neck length, slide the head onto the neck. Then pull the neck skin up to the head and attach the skin to the neck with pins. Now remove the head and move the skin about 1 inch farther up the neck and secure with pins. Slide the head onto the neck once again. This should be very close to a final position; adjust as needed. To help secure the head to the neck once a final position is chosen, apply hot glue within the artificial head shell. Quickly reattach the head before the glue begins to cool.

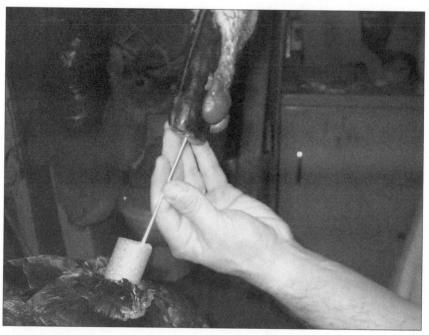

Attaching head.

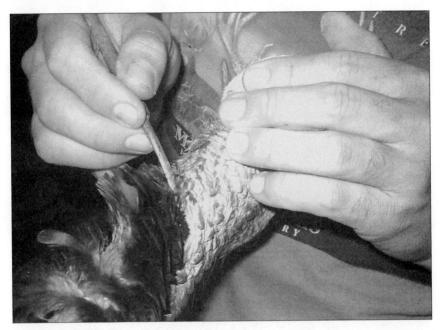

Tucking neck skin.

To attach a freeze-dried head, adjust the length of the artificial neck. Don't be hesitant about cutting the soft neck material from the enclosed wire. If you trim too much, it can be easily replaced. Be as accurate as possible when adjusting the length of the head and neck. (As discussed earlier, I would rather have the neck slightly short than slightly long.) After determining the proper neck length, insert the wire that is centered in the neck material into the center of the head manikin. This wire will support the head. Slide the head onto this wire until the head manikin meets the neck material. Now pull the skin to meet the head. If the length is correct, begin by pinning the uppermost portion of the skin that forms a V into place with about ¼ inch of overlap. Now turn your attention to the front of the head in the waddles area. Begin tucking the body skin under the waddles, and continue by tucking the skin upward on each side until the V in the very back is reached. Finish by tucking the skin at the V. Be careful not to damage any of these small fragile feathers. To groom this area, gently arrange these small feathers with a regulator or small wire.

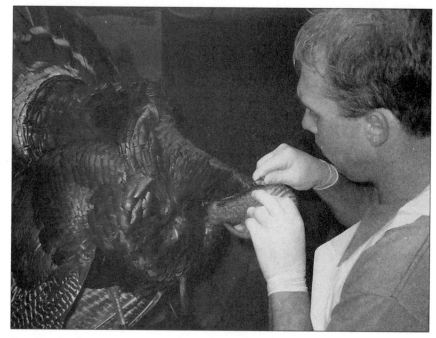

Strutting bird.

During the painting and attachment process, remember one thing: reference, reference, reference. Without reference photos your attempts will be frustrated by continual problems, but by taking your time and using your reference the head and its connection to the body will appear convincing and natural.

13

Base Building 101

At this point, you should be nearly ready to set your trophy aside and admire the fruits of your labor. First, the finishing touches must be applied. Attaching your trophy to an appropriate base will provide that finished look, but the base you choose will vary depending on the pose.

A flying bird will be placed on a panel or piece of driftwood—either now or during the mounting process—then hung on the wall. A breast mount will be mounted on a panel, and no extra work will be necessary, but a strutting or gobbling bird needs to be attached to a base similar to the habitat from which it came. I have seen a lot of standing or strutting birds attached to a piece of finished hardwood. Although this is quick and easy, I don't think it showcases the bird in a natural setting. Such a setting will add one last element that helps bring your mount to life.

To begin, you must think of the terrain or type of ground cover present in the area where the bird was taken. An excellent method for providing a natural-looking base is to start with a dirt base and build from there with leaves or pine needles, along with small flowers, pine cones, ferns, or other natural plant matter.

To begin making a natural base, you will need a piece of ½-inch plywood. It doesn't need to be treated because it will remain inside. Cut the plywood in an oval shape that measures roughly 32 by 15 inches. This measurement is a basic guideline and can be adjusted slightly either way. Continue by screwing a 20-inch length of 1 × 6 to the center. This completes your core. Place the holes for the leg wires now to avoid damaging the foam later. Hold the mounted bird over the wood and mark each area that is contacted by leg wires. Drill the holes with a drill bit slightly larger than the wire, and then add a base material.

Cutting the base plywood.

Several base materials are available, but one that is easy to use is two-part urethane foam. This is basically the same foam that is in the manikins we use for mounting. When you purchase this foam for base building it is in a liquid form. Mixing the two parts together creates a chemical reaction that causes the foam to expand, then harden. Instructions come with each kit, and they explain mixing directions along with what hazards to avoid.

Once the foam is mixed and begins to rise, it will become very hot and sticky. Because the foam can be hard to remove if you spill any or get any on your hands, I recommend wearing gloves and an apron and working carefully.

It may take a few tries to get used to the foam. Initially, you may use too much or not enough. A great guideline is to use the same size plywood each time and vary the formula slightly until you get just the right amount. This nearly eliminates waste.

Begin by laying the plywood core on a shallow bed of peat moss, which will prevent any other materials beneath the plywood from sticking.

Materials used for a dirt base.

Mixing the components.

The foam components have large names, so they are simply dubbed A and B. In a small container, pour a little of each in a ratio of almost one to one. Follow the directions exactly for good expansion and hardening. To mix the two-part foam, use a cordless drill with a wire in the chuck that has been shaped into the form of a **P**. Operate the drill slowly, mixing the liquids thoroughly until they begin to change colors and rise. The foam will become a very light tan color when it is ready.

It is usually best to make a base so that if some of the added particles fall free a light color won't show through. So to add color to the foam—prior to adding both liquids—pour in either A or B and then add "powdered tempera paint." A variety of colors are available, but for dirt scenes brown usually works the best. Now mix the powdered tempera thoroughly into the chosen liquid. When a uniform color is achieved, add the remaining component. Continue thoroughly mixing until the foam begins to rise.

It is beneficial to color the edges of the light-colored plywood.

In a pinch, a small amount of paint will work for coloring the light-colored foam.

Pour this rising mixture onto the plywood core. Once the foam is poured, it will be necessary to work quickly. Begin shifting the plywood from side to side and from front to back; this will evenly distribute the foam, resulting in a smooth surface.

After the foam has been spread evenly, sprinkle dry peat moss all over the foam base. Adding pine needles will enhance an otherwise plain base. Be careful not to touch the foam surface while applying these materials, though. The surface will remain sticky for several minutes before the foam begins to harden. Once it does, the dirt and most of the pine needles will be permanently attached. Let the base sit undisturbed until hard to the touch.

To prepare the base for attaching the turkey, insert a short length of wire the same size as the leg wire from the bottom through the preexisting holes. Push the wire straight through the foam, then gently wiggle to slightly widen the holes.

Hold the turkey by the legs and work each leg wire into the holes. It may take some maneuvering to find each hole, but be

Evenly pour on the quickly rising foam.

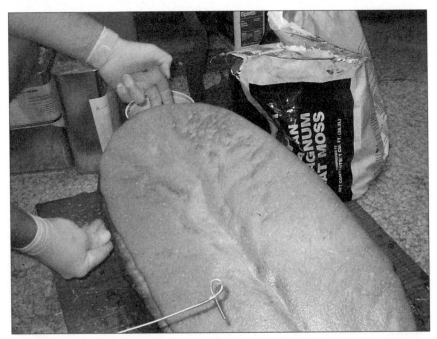

Then spread by tipping the plywood core forward to back and side to side.

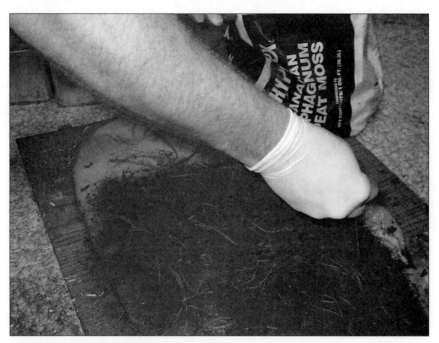

Attach any material, preferably that found in the area the trophy was taken.

patient and the wire will soon slide through. After the wire begins to slide in, push the feet flush with the base. With the feet firmly on the base, bend each wire to a 90-degree angle, parallel against the bottom of the base. Secure the turkey to the base by screwing 1½-inch screws next to the wire and through the same hole. This will firmly anchor the turkey. Finish by using a cut-off tool to trim the excess wire. Using the same tool, grind down any burr or sharp point that may protrude from the bottom of the base. The screws should be flush to the bottom, but if you would like to cover them, hot glue a small piece of felt to this area.

To further enhance the base, attach any spring flowers or other vegetation.

If you want to place a strutting or gobbling turkey on the wall the process of base preparation is simple. First, you will need to order a panel, and there are numerous designs available. If you choose a panel that is too large it will overpower the look of the bird, while one too small will look puny in comparison. An ideal size to start with is 16 by 20 inches. Now attach a hardwood limb in the center of the lower half of the panel. Dogwood or oak works

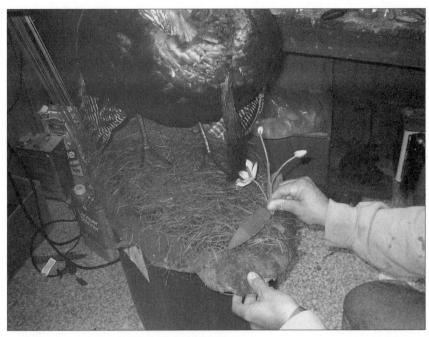

Attachment of items such as small flowers can greatly enhance a base, giving it a realistic springtime effect.

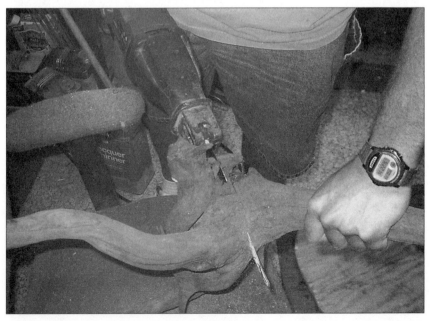

Adding driftwood can also enhance a mount.

great. Hardwood is preferable because once it dries, deterioration isn't a major problem. Secure the limb by pre-drilling the panel, then insert three 2½-inch screws and tighten.

To position the bird properly, mark the middle of the limb, then drill holes 2½-inches on either side of that mark. Ideally, the holes will be just slightly larger than the leg wires.

To finish installation, slide the leg wires through the holes and cut the excess flush with the bottom of the limb. Slightly lift the turkey's feet from the limb, apply some five-minute epoxy to the wires and a small section of the foot, and then return the feet to the limb. This locks the turkey into place. Hide the bottom holes by coloring the wire ends or glue a piece of bark over each hole. You can dress things up further by adding some artificial leaves to the junction of the limb and panel.

PAINTING THE LEGS AND FEET

While it would be nice to be able to finish the feet along with head painting and attachment, you must wait until immediately prior to the permanent attachment of bird to base before doing so. The reason we need to wait until now to paint the feet is that they were not dry in the initial mounting stage. After the mount dries for two to three weeks, the legs will be dry enough to gauge the perfect amount of paint.

As the legs dry they shrink a small amount and lose color. Some birds lose more color than others, and the amount of color lost depends on the preservation method chosen.

Finishing the legs is very simple. Start by misting the entire scaled area with pure white. Be careful not to color the black toenails or the feathers at the knee joint. It is important that you mist very lightly; you should only notice a minimal color shift. Now mist over the top of the white with a dark red. Again, mist a small amount at a time until you have a color close to the reference you are using. When you have the correct shade, apply a satin or basecoat sealer to the legs.

Congratulations, you should now have a trophy that will provide many years, if not a lifetime, of fond memories.

CHAPTER 14

Care of Your Trophy

By now, all of your research, hard work, and equipment investments should have paid off in some way. The fruits of your labor may have resulted in a cape or fan, or you may have completed several mounts. Either way, you are going to want the artwork you have created to be around for many years. In great part, this depends on whether the owner possesses the knowledge to properly care for and clean the trophy.

All too often I have customers come in and begin complaining about the mount completed by their last taxidermist. As I am always curious about the methods of other taxidermists, I usually begin asking for details. Many times the conversation reveals the fact that the previous deer or turkey mount only lasted four or five years before it began to deteriorate rapidly. After further investigation, I find that the mount in question has been placed near or over a heat source. This is a very poor location for a mount of any kind. The only person at fault in this scenario is the owner who didn't take time to learn the dos and don'ts of mount care.

The guidelines I recommend are simple and easy to follow. A major rule for prolonging the life of a mount is to keep it away from a direct heat source. When the mount is subjected to extreme temperature changes it quickly breaks down due to the corresponding expansion and shrinkage that take place. When the mount is kept in an environment with a consistent temperature and then exposed to a sudden warming, the skin will inevitably expand. Then, as the temperature falls back to normal, the skin shrinks.

If the heat happens to be a dry heat, such as that from an electric heat source, the problems seem to compound because any moisture that exists will be pulled from the mount. The moisture that remains in a preserved skin should be minute, but it is essential. When that small balance of moisture is virtually eliminated, the mount will become more like a potato chip than a healthy, preserved skin. This severe drying will eventually cause cracking and other damage.

Another element that creates a harmful environment for a mount is too much moisture. Many times the hunter will return to his home with a beautiful mount only to find it relegated to the basement or garage. This directive usually comes from a non-hunting spouse who doesn't understand a hunter's desire to properly preserve, store, and display his or her trophy. There is only one method to combat this: Try to get your spouse involved in some of your outdoor adventures. Be assured that if you introduce someone to the outdoors they will soon appreciate the beauty of most any wildlife art.

Not long ago I had a visit from a customer who needed help with a problem. The hunter told of an unbelievable elk hunt that he was fortunate enough to take. After several days of trekking rugged mountains, he earned the opportunity to harvest a trophy bull. One well-placed shot later and the hunter bagged his dream elk. He was careful to follow good field-care guidelines and prep the skin for the return home.

After his hunt, he visited a local taxidermist and arranged to have his trophy preserved. Months passed as he eagerly waited for the day he could take his mount home. Finally, he made the trip to the taxidermist and picked up his trophy. The bull happened to be a 6 × 6 that scored around 320, easily the trophy of a lifetime. When he got it home, however, his wife adamantly objected to having this beautiful creature grace any wall of a home in which she lived.

To avoid serious domestic problems the hunter placed his trophy in an outside utility building. Throughout the year, the humidity and temperature within the brick building fluctuated like a yo-yo.

In three short years the tear ducts and nose pad began to crack. Needless to say, the mount was ruined. And all this was due to a lack of knowledge on the part of the hunter and a lack of consideration from a non-hunting spouse. Had he understood the effects of temperature and moisture, the hunter could have at least placed the mount in a more stable environment at a friend's house.

An ideal environment for a mount is similar to the comfort range for humans. Also, stability in both temperature and humidity is vital.

Another major issue is the effect the sun can have on a mount. Direct sunlight is detrimental to almost everything. Leave a piece of plastic in direct sunlight for a year or two, then test its integrity. It will probably crumble easily. This damage is also apparent when viewing taxidermy pieces that have been placed in direct sunlight. The usual results are cracks due to regular heating and cooling. Another dead giveaway of sun damage is the severe fading that eventually takes place.

This is easily avoided, of course, by simply choosing a better location for displaying the mount. If possible, situate the trophy away from any large, south-facing windows. If this is the only available area, try to restrict the sunlight with window blinds or curtains. This will help tremendously.

Although controlling a mount's environment is 99 percent of caring for it, there may eventually be a problem with a broken feather or body part. This may result from the mount falling from a wall, or a child or pet may cause the damage while playing. Like most works of art, a mount is fragile, so it is always a good idea to locate it in an out of the way area. But sometimes things just happen.

Probably the easiest problem to repair is a broken feather. The primary tail and wing feathers are the most noticeable, as well as the most vulnerable. Once a mount is dry these feathers are usually very hard to pluck from the remaining tissue. If a feather breaks, find the section that has been snapped off. To reattach the feather, simply slide a small gauge wire into the quill of the feather. The size of the wire for this job will vary with the placement of the break and the size of the feather. Try to fit the feather with a wire that will fill most of the quill. Next, place a small amount of super glue on the wire and slide it into the quill. Repeat the procedure with the other end of the wire and the remaining portion of feather. Adjust the fit as needed, and this repair should go unnoticed. If the area of the break is too small to insert a wire, use only super glue.

Unfortunately, more severe damage does occasionally occur. If a major area is broken, such as the head or a wing, all is not lost. Repairs can be made, but they may not be as easily hidden as a

Dust a turkey frequently, as they eagerly collect airborne dirt.

feather repair. With a major break, the area may be somewhat reluctant to resume its original position.

To repair a severe break of any kind, use wire, pins, and super glue to reattach the parts. Because areas such as the head and wings have already been wired, simply positioning the damaged area back in its original location may be all it takes to fix the problem. You can further strengthen the affected area by using glue and pins to permanently affix the skin that was torn free. If you proceed carefully, and the repair area is properly groomed, the damaged area may be totally concealed.

Barring major care issues, a turkey still needs to be dusted on a regular basis. A vacuum can be used when dusting a mammal mount, but don't try this on a bird mount, as it can easily damage and/or change the position of feathers.

Because feathers readily attract and hold dust, a quality duster is necessary. I like to use a commercially-made duster with synthetic fibers. Just swipe the bird gently, brushing with the grain of the feathers. Do this every other week and dust accumulation will be eliminated.

With proper care and an ideal environment, there is every reason to believe your trophy will last a lifetime.

CHAPTER 15

Tips for Achieving a Better Mount

Choose the Correct Manikin

Choosing the right manikin for your mount may seem elementary—and it should be. But it seems that many novice and trained taxidermists insist on using a form that is too large for their turkey. The thought process seems to be that bigger is better. This is far from the truth.

Several different manikins are available on the market; some use weight to determine an accurate size, while others use length and circumference. I have found both methods accurate. Which size indicator you choose matters much less than taking an accurate measurement. Also, if in doubt, choose a size smaller, especially if you are on the low end of the measurements. For example, if you have a 19-pound bird and you can choose from a manikin sculpted for a 17- to 19-pound bird or one sculpted for a 19- to 21-pound bird, it will be much easier to work with the smaller manikin.

Repairing Bent or Broken Feathers

Unfortunately, bent or broken feathers occur all too frequently. I discussed fixing broken feathers with wire and super glue in the last chapter, but it will be helpful to know how to deal with similar situations that arise during the harvesting of your bird or during the mounting process. Sometimes such damage is unavoidable, whether from the shot itself or from a flapping bird or from accidentally placing something on top of the bird while it is in the freezer. The only thing we can do is prevent as much damage as possible.

Once the damage is done, however, we need to repair the affected area. Obviously, some areas are more easily repaired than others. Any feather damage can be detrimental to a mount, but it seems that the wing and tail primaries are the most noticeable. Usually, you will only have to deal with one or two of these.

To make a repair on either a wing or tail primary it is best to mount the turkey as usual and let dry. After the turkey is fully dry, pull the damaged feather from the bird and replace it with an identical feather from another bird, using super glue to lock the feather into place. If you don't have access to a replacement feather, pluck the broken feather before the mounting process and position the remaining feathers so that they hide the empty space.

Occasionally, I have turkeys brought in that have curved tail feathers. This is from placing the bird in the freezer without much thought being given to these fragile feathers. After being bent for any length of time, these feathers are sometimes difficult to straighten. The first thing you should do, of course, is try to avoid this situation, but if it occurs it can be corrected. After properly cleaning the tail, place it in a pan of hot water. Let the tail sit for 30 minutes, then remove it and let it dry. This should relax the feathers enough to relieve the problem.

DEALING WITH LARGER DAMAGED AREAS

If a damaged area is much larger than just a few feathers, more drastic measures must be taken. As stated in the chapter on field care, it is usually best to determine the pose in which you'd like to mount your trophy before pulling the trigger. However, if the shot does severe damage to the breast, for example, a flying mount with the breast to the wall might be more suitable than a strutting gobbler. If heavy damage is done to just one side, you may choose to hide the damage by mounting the bird gobbling and place him on a limb hanging from the wall. If the back feathers are damaged, you may opt for a breast mount.

There are also methods of completely replacing entire feather tracts, but this is definitely for the more advanced taxidermist. Keep in mind that nothing is a lost cause. By using the knowledge acquired from this book, you should be able to determine some method for preserving your prize.

PROPERLY DEGREASE, CLEAN, AND DRY THE SKIN

These matter has been covered thoroughly in the chapters on field care, skinning, fleshing, and degreasing, but they can't be stressed enough. You will find that many of the problems you encounter can be reduced or eliminated by carefully following the guidelines for these procedures.

BRING THE MOUNT TO LIFE WITH ACTION

Precise head and neck positioning can breathe life into an average mount. It seems that most novice taxidermists are hesitant to put much movement into their mounts. A good example of this is straight necks and heads or rigid, evenly placed legs. But a mount that portrays movement can be very convincing. Start by putting some bend into the head and neck area. This goes for any portion of the body that can be moved for the desired pose while maintaining a natural look. A mount that I recently had the opportunity to see illustrates this point perfectly. The turkey was in full strut while gobbling. The mount itself wasn't particularly impressive, but the head was positioned to one side and really seemed to bring the mount to life.

Another example is the legs. Unless you are mounting your bird on a limb, it does wonders to place a standing or strutting bird with one leg in front of the other. This simple positioning gives the illusion of movement and, therefore, life.

As you loosen up, learn more, and gain confidence you will quickly understand what it takes to re-create wildlife accurately.

DRY THE FEET ON THE SURFACE WHERE THEY WILL BE PERMANENTLY ATTACHED

As you learn the art of taxidermy you will quickly find yourself paying more attention to detail. A detail overlooked by some taxidermist is the attachment of the feet to the base. It is a pet peeve of mine to see an otherwise quality mount attached to a limb with a completely open, flat foot. A bird could never hang on naturally with these flat feet. To look natural, which is always our goal, the feet should conform to the surface to which they are mounted. When you see feet that don't conform to the base, you can bet the taxidermist allowed the bird to dry on one surface then attached it to another.

To avoid this problem it is usually best to prepare the base prior to mounting and then attach the bird. In cases where you intend to attach the turkey to a flat surface, you can usually get away with temporarily attaching the feet to a piece of plywood before transferring the bird to the finished base later on. When the final perch is to be a limb, however, the best advice is to attach the turkey while it remains flexible. Tack each toe down securely to simulate a turkey gripping the limb in a natural way.

Touch Up the Hairs with Mascara

If you have chosen an artificial head touching up hair won't be a problem. If you decided to paint a freeze-dried head yourself, you may wonder how you are going to remove the paint from the many fine hairs on the natural turkey head once you've finished. You would

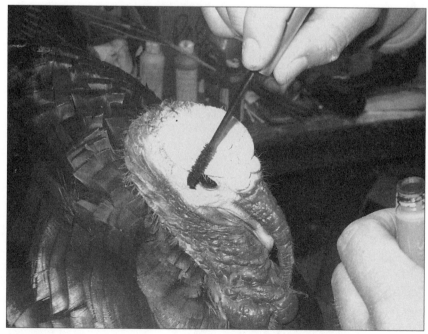

Head painting.

have to go to great pains to actually remove the paint from these hairs, potentially ruining the job you just finished, but you do have another option for restoring them to their original color—mascara.

You may want to purchase a tube just for this job, as the lady of the house might have problems with your using her mascara on a turkey head. If you are the lady of the house, you have a distinct advantage over the rest of us who are mascara ignorant. I haven't experimented a great deal with this, but I am sure certain brands will go on with less residue than others. To achieve the most natural-looking coverage you may want to try several different varieties.

To apply the mascara, very lightly brush it on the fine hairs and the small hair-like feathers that protect the ears. Be careful not to get any black on the head itself.

BE SELF-CONFIDENT

In talking to other taxidermists, whether they have years of experience or are just learning a new technique, it seems that the biggest disadvantage isn't lack of knowledge but the lack of confidence. Confidence can make the difference between a person who tries and quits and one who completes a given task. All taxidermists have gone through the same learning stages, the frustrations, the doubts. I can assure you that the taxidermist who wins next year's state, national, or even world championship is struggling today to produce his best work. I can also assure you that his first attempt won't be remotely similar to the one that clinches the championship.

When the going gets tough and you feel like taxidermy isn't for you, just quit—but not for good. After a short break to gather your thoughts or let your temper cool, step up to the plate and continue. Things will get easier, and your work will improve with every bit of experience you gain. When it's all finished you will have the satisfaction that comes with completing something you have worked hard to achieve.

JOIN YOUR STATE TAXIDERMY ASSOCIATION

Joining a state taxidermy association can give the learning process a tremendous boost. Taxidermy associations nationwide hold annual taxidermy seminars and competitions. These events are geared toward improving the techniques and craftsmanship of the organization's members.

Years ago, taxidermy was basically a secret art. No books were written, no videos available, and you wouldn't have even thought of asking the taxidermist down the street for instruction. But times have changed in a big way, and joining a state taxidermy association can put you a phone call away from the years of wisdom and experience gained by fellow taxidermists in your area. Most are eager to provide how-to instruction to a fellow member. This is especially true if they know you are new to the art.

Competitions are also a tremendous learning tool. During the competitions some of the best taxidermists in the world are asked to critique each mount that has been entered. This is invaluable, as they not only critique your work, but elaborate on ways to improve it.

SUBSCRIBE TO A TAXIDERMY MAGAZINE

Subscribing to *Taxidermy Today* or *Breakthrough* magazine can be a tremendous asset to the budding taxidermist. Although these publications are not geared solely towards turkey taxidermy, they usually have at least a section devoted to birds, if not specifically the wild turkey, in every issue. Articles written for these publications contain the most advanced procedures found anywhere.

To subscribe to *Breakthrough,* call 1-800-783-7266. To contact *Taxidermy Today,* call 1-800-851-7955.

INDEX